"*Thriving Despite a Difficult Marr[iage]* ...[li]fe in spite of an unfulfilling marriag[e] ...[suffer]ing and mere surviving to finding j[oy] ...[In] the hands of master soul physicians such as Misja and Misja, the hidden chambers of the heart come alive with wisdom for living. Their practical theology of desire, their explanation of the battlefield of the soul, and their relational process for moving from hoping in your marriage to hoping in God are worth the proverbial price of the book. *Thriving Despite a Difficult Marriage* is for any spouse who wants to love well, hope endlessly, and rejoice deeply—despite external circumstances and relational disappointments."

—ROBERT W. KELLEMEN, PhD, chairman of the master of arts in Christian counseling and discipleship department, Capital Bible Seminary; founder, RPM Ministries

"A profound yet simple message of hope that will enable Christians in difficult marriages to be committed to their spouses but free to live their own lives. It is rare to see such good material that addresses the complex relationship and scriptural dynamics of difficult marriages. Chuck and Mike Misja obviously have a wealth of experience and insight to offer those who feel trapped in their difficult marriages."

—KARLA DOWNING, MA, licensed marriage and family therapist; author of *10 Lifesaving Principles for Women in Difficult Marriages* and *When Love Hurts*

"On your wedding day, you hoped and dreamed of happily ever after. You never imagined that marriage could bring the heartache and regrets you have experienced, and you are now at a place where hope is lost. You've given up trying to fix your spouse or even yourself. If this describes you, you have found the right book. Authors Mike and Chuck Misja will challenge you to see your situation and your spouse through the eternal perspective of how a loving Father desires to refine you even as you experience disappointment and hardship."

—DR. JULI SLATTERY, family psychologist, Focus on the Family

"This book does not pretend marriage is easy. But Michael and Chuck Misja have cleared a new path through the thorny issues of marital disappointment, challenging spouses to follow God into the pain and learn to live with radical honesty, transcendent purpose, heroic effort, and unquenchable hope. Their words offer deep and lasting joy to those who will embrace and persevere in a difficult marriage by God's grace."

—NANCY GROOM, author of *From Bondage to Bonding*

Thriving Despite a
Difficult
Marriage

Michael Misja, PhD
& Chuck Misja, PhD

NAVPRESS

NAVPRESS🄰

NavPress is the publishing ministry of The Navigators, an international Christian organization and leader in personal spiritual development. NavPress is committed to helping people grow spiritually and enjoy lives of meaning and hope through personal and group resources that are biblically rooted, culturally relevant, and highly practical.

For a free catalog go to www.NavPress.com
or call 1.800.366.7788 in the United States or 1.800.839.4769 in Canada.

ISBN-13: 978-1-60006-214-8

Cover design by David Uttley, TheDesignWorks Group,
    www.thedesignworksgroup.com
Cover image by Max Delson, iStock

Some of the anecdotal illustrations in this book are true to life and are included with the permission of the persons involved. All other illustrations are composites of real situations, and any resemblance to people living or dead is coincidental.

Unless otherwise identified, all Scripture quotations in this publication are taken from The *Holy Bible, English Standard Version* (ESV), copyright © 2001 by Crossway Bibles, a division of Good News Publishers. Used by permission. All rights reserved. Other versions used include: *THE MESSAGE* (MSG). Copyright © 1993, 1994, 1995, 1996, 2000, 2001, 2002. Used by permission of NavPress Publishing Group; *GOD'S WORD* is a copyrighted work of God's Word to the Nations. Quotations are used by permission. Copyright 1995 by God's Word to the Nations. All rights reserved; and the King James Version.

Library of Congress Cataloging-in-Publication Data

Misja, Michael, 1950-
Thriving despite a difficult marriage / Michael Misja and Chuck Misja.
    p. cm.
Includes bibliographical references.
ISBN 978-1-60006-214-8
1. Marriage--Religious aspects--Christianity. 2. Conflict management--Religious aspects--Christianity. I. Misja, Chuck, 1948- II. Title.
BV835.M594 2008
248.8'44--dc22

2008046163

Printed in the United States of America

3 4 5 6 7 8 / 13 12 11 10 09

This book is dedicated to our parents, Charley and Verna Misja,
whose marriage of fifty-two years modeled not only how to
thrive in a difficult marriage but also how to have
love and joy "until death do you part."

Contents

Foreword   9

Acknowledgments   11

To Our Readers   13

PART 1: DIFFICULT MARRIAGES
When Divorce Is Not an Option

CHAPTER 1: Three Paths for Difficult Marriages   17

CHAPTER 2: Why Marriages Are Difficult   39

PART 2: THE HEART OF A MARRIAGE
Darkness and Light

CHAPTER 3: The Desiring Heart   59

CHAPTER 4: Difficult Spouses   81

CHAPTER 5: Corrupted Desires   99

CHAPTER 6: Dangerous Spouses   117

PART 3: WHEN IT ALL GOES WRONG
Coming to Grips with the Loss

CHAPTER 7: The Wounded Heart   139

CHAPTER 8: The Surviving Heart   157

PART 4: TRANSCENDING SUFFERING
Thriving Despite

CHAPTER 9: Freedom and Disengagement   173

CHAPTER 10: The Thriving Heart   193

Notes   215

About the Authors   217

Foreword

On your wedding day, you hoped and dreamed of happily ever after. You never imagined that marriage could bring the heartache and regrets you have experienced. Along your journey, you have dared to believe in various panaceas and formulas that promised to breathe life into your loveless marriage. Yet each conference and book and counselor seemed only to deepen your desperation. You are now at a place where hope is lost. You've given up trying to fix your spouse or even yourself. You are through with seeking advice and tired of being the only one working at your marriage.

If this describes you, you have found the right book. Dr. Mike Misja and Dr. Chuck Misja do not promise to fix your marriage or even give you hope of renewed love. They also do not pander to the relativistic message of many psychologists that you have tried your best and should throw in the towel. Instead, they will encourage you with a broader message of the purpose of life, marriage, and disappointment.

Over the course of twenty years, Mike and Chuck have met with hundreds of men and women flailing in the wake of disappointment and devastation in marriage. Some of them are married to abusive spouses, some to spouses with mental or physical illnesses, and still others to spouses who simply don't care. While holding to the permanence of marriage, Mike and Chuck also recognize that it is not enough simply to tell someone to endure the constant rejection and agony of an unhealthy marriage. They also recognize that not every marriage can be restored to a fulfilling and loving union.

Through this book, they will explore with you what it looks like to thrive as a person in spite of the great difficulty of an unfulfilling and even hurtful marriage. This book will challenge you to see your situation and your spouse through an eternal perspective of how a loving Father desires to refine you, even as you experience disappointment and hardship.

— DR. JULI SLATTERY, PsyD, Family Psychologist,
Focus on the Family

Acknowledgments

This book is a result of talking with hundreds of couples who have struggled in difficult marriages. We are privileged to be part of their journeys toward healing and wholeness or toward thriving despite ongoing difficulties. They have challenged us with their painful struggles and taught us with wisdom that can come only from a sincere pursuit of God.

Many wise counselors, pastors, and friends have stimulated our thoughts and brought godly perspectives to this work. We are most grateful to our original think tank of colleagues from North Coast Family Foundation who got up far too early in the morning to meet and wrestle with how to thrive in a difficult marriage. Joe Koch, Caroline Stanczak, Liz Shella, and JoAnn Shade were willing to engage in challenging, loving, and sometimes contentious exchanges on differing perspectives concerning why marriages are difficult and what God wants from someone living with a spouse who is destructive and not likely to change. We are thankful to them for the courage to go through the dark forest of gender perspectives, finding a way to include male and female differences without alienating many we were trying to help.

We want to express our deep appreciation to Dr. JoAnn Shade, who spent many hours helping us refine and articulate the concepts of this book. Her willingness to read through chapters and provide feedback, especially in the final push to meet the deadline, was invaluable. She has been a wonderful colleague and wise contributor to this book. Her belief that it should be written and that God wanted us to write it provided us inspiration and hope that God will use this book to help his people.

The counselors at North Coast Family Foundation have been helpful in listening to ideas and offering their experience and wisdom. In addition to our think tank, we are grateful to Mark Yoder, Sara Fellows, Susan Weber, Nancy Berger, and Mary Alexander.

I, Mike, am especially appreciative to the men in my pastors' support group with whom I have regularly met for the past ten years. Tom Petersburg (and his wife, JoAnn), Rick Duncan, George Mercado, Joe Abraham, Juri Ammari, Bob Kuntz, Randy Chestnut, Jeff Thompson, Bob Mackey, and Doug Davidson have all been challenging and encouraging, asking the tough questions every man should be asked. Other pastors, especially Ryan Edlund, Jonathon Schaeffer, Mickey Aquilino, and Russel DeBord have graciously offered their biblical and pastoral wisdom on how to help those struggling with difficult marriages.

We are thankful to NavPress and our editor, Tracey Lawrence, for guiding us through the long process of getting a book from the infant stage to publication. We appreciate their willingness to publish a book that is not in the mainstream of Christian thought for marriage counseling, yet will bring hope to many in struggling marriages.

We could not have done this without the gracious understanding and encouragement of our families. Our children, Olivia, Emily, Carmen, and ChesseMei (Mike), and Chuck, Matt, and Jeanette (Chuck) have believed in this work and been wonderfully supportive.

Our deepest gratitude is to our wives, Lin and Jackie, who have spent a combined total approaching seventy years married to and loving Misja men, one of the most complex and difficult breed of husbands to grace this earth (we love you, Dad, as you "chortle"-laugh with joy from heaven).

We are most profoundly grateful to God, whose deep, deep love for struggling saints provides the hope that is found in this book.

— MIKE and CHUCK

To Our Readers

As you read this book, you will be going on a journey that may lead you out of the darkness of despair and into the light of hope. *Thriving Despite a Difficult Marriage* has been written in a way that parallels the counseling process. Each chapter, like every counseling session, builds upon the last. While you may read and understand the last chapters without having read the previous ones, you will not benefit from them unless you have built the foundation found in earlier chapters. If your counseling is to last ten sessions, the healing and hope from the last two meetings will emerge from the hard work done in the previous eight. So enjoy the journey. We pray that God will bless you and teach you to thrive even if your marriage remains difficult.

— MIKE and CHUCK

PART I

Difficult Marriages

WHEN DIVORCE IS NOT AN OPTION

CHAPTER I

Three Paths for Difficult Marriages

Nevertheless such shall have trouble.
— *1 Corinthians 7:28, KJV*

Divorce is not an option, so misery seems inevitable. It's just not working out. Nothing is changing. No matter what you do, no matter what you say, he doesn't get it. In spite of your doing everything she has asked of you, she is still angry and distant. Hope has taken the last train out of town, and you are faced with some tough days ahead.

IS IT EVER OKAY TO GIVE UP ON YOUR MARRIAGE?

You're where you thought you'd never be. You thought if you did it the right way—you know, followed the rules and all that—your marriage was going to work, and you'd be happy. Happily ever after. Yeah, right. No one told you you'd be as miserable as you are. The marriage journey is tough, isn't it? You started well, but now you're living with a broken heart, feeling trapped in a difficult marriage without hope, and you don't even want to begin to think about the future. *What future?* Every morning you wake up in disbelief and every night you go to bed in despair. *Is this my marriage? Has it really come to this?*

It's not like you haven't tried, is it? You've gone to the seminars that teach helpful principles and techniques on how to build a strong marriage. The ideas you learned made a lot of sense to you, and it seemed like your marriage was headed in the right direction. You even had a few warm moments with your spouse that made it seem like things were going to be different. But you were merely teased with hope because nothing really changed. Two months, weeks, or even days after the marriage conference you're back to the same old patterns. The bickering and coldness have returned, and you feel more discouraged than ever. You're not able to run away from the reality that your marriage is empty.

If you're strong enough to look beyond your pain, way down inside yourself, what disturbs you more is what's happening to your heart. Every once in a while, when you take that honest look, you are appalled at the dark, wild thoughts you have. You never thought you could have such ugly thoughts about your "beloved." Your heart is being polluted with bitterness or is hardening with smug disdain for your spouse. You might even be so lonely and empty that you are allowing yourself to be drawn to someone else. So not only is your marriage in bad shape, but your heart is a mess too.

> *Q: "Everybody tells me I'm supposed to hang in there and believe that if I trust and do what I should, my marriage is going to turn around. I want to scream, 'You don't understand! Nothing helps. Why should I keep trying?'"*

Is it ever okay to give up on your marriage? A lot of people think so. The fighting, game playing, or loneliness has destroyed the relationship, and sooner or later a spouse decides to get out while he or she still has some self-respect. So the couple divorces. Some couples do it legally, but many more divorce emotionally, staying married while living separate, distant lives. Either way, the marriage is over. Others who are in a destructive, messy marriage stay together and slug it out with each other like two fighters trapped in a marathon cage fight, scratching and clawing until neither is left standing. They don't divorce, but they'd bleed a lot less if they did.

Q: *"Doesn't it make sense to admit my relationship can't be fixed and it's better to cut my losses and run?"*

We have talked with hundreds of couples who have struggled in difficult marriages. This is a tough, sincere question many people ask us on a regular basis. As Christian psychologists, we believe in a tough, though often unpopular, answer: Unless there is a pattern of abuse or unchanging immorality, the answer is "No, it's *not* better to give up on your marriage." Instead, never quit, never give up, don't stop praying and searching for a way to turn your marriage around. Miracles happen, people change, and, besides, you don't know what God has planned for your marriage. In addition, you can't give up on your marriage without betraying your heart. In the best part of your heart, you will always hope that love will come back to life and your marriage will get better.

Q: *"But what if it doesn't? I can't imagine wasting even more years trying to fix this debacle only to end up even more miserable than I am now. If giving up on my marriage isn't an option, then am I supposed to try even harder?"*

Trying harder seems to make sense. After all, you have been taught to believe that anything can be fixed through prayer, hard work, and determination. So why not dig in, do what you're supposed to do, and work even harder to get your marriage on track? Another workshop, CD, prayer session — there must be something you can find that will turn your marriage around. "But," you tell yourself, "I've done this all before and have gotten the same dismal result: Nothing really changes." You are tired, frustrated, becoming cynical, and leery about getting all excited over a new book or teaching on marriage, fearful of ending up even more disillusioned.

Q: "Are you saying that I may have to start thinking that my spouse will never change and start accepting that my marriage may always be difficult?"

Absolutely! The reality is that some spouses never change, and some marriages don't get better. While you can't ever give up hope, you don't want to keep banging your head into a brick wall trying to fix something that won't be fixed. There is a time when you should accept that the wall is there and that you don't have a way to tear it down. You may be in a tough marriage that is not likely to improve, and, if you aren't wise, it could destroy you.

Q: "Okay, if I can't give up on my marriage and trying harder to fix it does not change anything, what options do I have?"

We're glad you asked. There is another way besides giving up or trying harder: Learn how to *thrive* and live well even if your marriage remains difficult and your spouse never changes. The ache and confusion you are experiencing can be faced and worked through so you can have a life of meaning and contentment even if your relationship with your husband or wife remains painful. You can live in an imperfect or difficult marriage and flourish. This is a book of hope for those who have difficult marriages and have worked hard to make them better, but are coming to the realization that their marriages are not going to change.

Sometimes people need permission to acknowledge what is true about their marriage—that it may never have a happy ending or a resolution that is satisfying. Disappointment, shame, and inferiority dominate the spirit of the individual who can't resolve the difficulties of an imperfect marriage. They often live lives of defeat, emptiness, and spiritual despair. But it doesn't have to be that way. It's possible to become equipped to thrive despite the lack of hope in your marriage. Most marriage teachings state that if certain steps or techniques are practiced, a happy, fulfilling marriage will result. Learning relational skills and applying spiritual principles are offered as solutions that will fix any marriage. Yet realistically, many individuals have worked hard at their marriage with little change. People need another way to view their situation in order to find a different sort of hope.

CHRISTIANS AND "GREAT MARRIAGES"

Q: "But aren't Christians supposed to have great marriages?"

In some ways we believe the current evangelical Christian culture does a disservice to married couples without knowing it. You see, we are caught up in a culture that truly believes any obstacle can be overcome. We can be successful at whatever we do if we just pray, put our minds to it, and push on toward our goals. We acknowledge struggle and talk about it as being part of the Christian life. We may read the book of Jeremiah and acknowledge that things didn't get better for the suffering prophet, or we may weep with compassion when we hear stories of persecution on the mission field. Yet when we encounter a struggler in our churches, we're often impatient and smugly condescending. We think, *Come on, get over it. You have all the stuff you need to get it together, so stop moaning and get happy.* This is especially true with our understanding of marriage. Those facing trials in their marriages are seen as having something wrong with them, while those who have marriages that seem to work are thought to have more spiritual maturity. Many couples learn to be dishonest about what is really going on in their marriages because no one else seems to wrestle and struggle as much as they do. If they speak up about their problems, they're afraid they'll be offered another book on the godly husband or the servant wife. These couples often feel that if they continue to struggle, it will be obvious to all that they simply aren't applying God's principles to their marriage. So they learn to put on a good show and hide the truth that they are just getting by, trying to survive in a painful marriage.

Some mature marriages result from two people developing the skills and selflessness needed to address the hard issues in their relationship. These marriages are a result of honest work and sacrificial love and are filled with transparency, humility, and honesty. They, indeed, have a depth of maturity that serves as a positive model. Other marriages that are held up as models of maturity may involve people who are just easy to get along with, who *fit* well with each other. As one pastor told us, "I understand difficult marriages and feel compassion for couples in pain. But I can't relate because my wife is so open with me. I don't have to work hard at it—love just overflows from my heart."

People in relationships without conflict are often happy to just go with the flow. These individuals may be easy to love or considered to be low-maintenance people. They may see the glass as half full and with their positive personality never get drawn into unpleasant conflicts. Their good relationships may not be the result of painstaking work on the difficult issues of marriage but the product of an easygoing personality style. These individuals often have smooth-running, good-looking marriages. But we run into confusion when we hold up marriages with low-maintenance, uncomplicated people as the models for godly, mature relationships.

Marriages between two thirsty, passionate souls who are selfish by nature tend to have conflicts and troubles. People are complex. Many people who are understood to be high-maintenance may be hard to love. High-maintenance people are often difficult in their personality styles and a challenge to relate to. They are too sensitive and notice every slight, or they're stubborn, insensitive, and unaware of their painful effects on others. They may be demanding, needy, moody, insecure, always discontent, bored, or adrenaline junkies.

Some high-maintenance spouses can also be a challenge because they don't settle for the ordinary; they desire lots of interaction and exhaust their mates with their passion for living. However, in reality, others are unkind, unloving people. They may be seen as destructive spouses. If you are such a person, or are married to such a person, and you want a stress-free marriage, you may be continually frustrated.

Scripture teaches us that marriage is inherently difficult. If we think of the relationship between God and the Hebrew people as a marriage, then we see God coping with a difficult, contentious spouse in a difficult marriage filled with tragedy and heartache. Christ, the bridegroom, was a man who was filled with sorrow and grief (see Isaiah 53) and suffered brutal rejection at the hands of his "beloved." The difficulties between Christ and his bride (the church) were so severe that his death was required in order for their relationship to be possible. Christ knew the difficulty of marriage.

For example, in Matthew 19 Christ gives his understanding:

Jesus' disciples objected [to his words], "If those are the terms of marriage, we're stuck. Why get married?"

But Jesus said, "Not everyone is mature enough to live a married life. It requires a certain aptitude and grace. Marriage isn't for everyone. Some, from birth seemingly, never give marriage a thought. Others never get asked—or accepted. And some decide not to get married for kingdom reasons. But if you're capable of growing into the largeness of marriage, do it." (Matthew 19:10-12, MSG)

Jesus made it clear that marriage would be costly and require much. The disciples were thinking the way we do: It doesn't make sense to be married if you aren't happy. Jesus challenged their thinking and told them marriage is not for the fragile. *Unhappiness is not the basis for ending a marriage.* He shattered their thinking that marriage wasn't worth the time and effort if it didn't result in happiness.

Difficult marriages are more the norm than the exception. This is what Paul said when he wrote that we would face many troubles in marriage (see 1 Corinthians 7:28). The word *trouble* is rendered as tribulation in other places. A literal understanding is that those who are married will undergo severe tribulation. The idea that all trouble and struggle can be eliminated from marriage is *not* biblical. Married couples are desperate for someone to acknowledge that it's okay for them to have ongoing struggles.

Q: *"You mean I can have a life even if I don't resolve all the stuff between me and my spouse? My difficult marriage doesn't make me the failure of the century? I'm not the Wicked Witch of the West because I sometimes wish I had not gotten married?"*

Many people we counsel believe they are failures and displeasing to God because their marriage is troubled. Most are already in enough pain and don't need to go through unnecessary shame and guilt. It's sometimes hard to accept that you can be whole even if your marriage isn't. Part of the reason for this is that most people don't have an understanding of how to live in a difficult marriage.

HOPE

Visiting Dom in the cancer ward was more difficult than I (Mike) imagined it would be. As I got off the elevator, I recognized the contrasting messages the hall conveyed. Bright, cheerful pictures were posted next to a closed door with the somber message, "Radiation in use. No visitors." The hospital made attempts to communicate that life was good while the scent of death and decay was unavoidable.

When I saw Dom shuffling down the hall, his frail body and lifeless eyes took me back sixteen years to another cancer ward. The eyes that haunted me then were those of our kid brother.

Mark was twenty-eight years old when cancer stole life from his body. My family's hearts were crushed during his battle. We prayed, hoped, and begged God to restore his life as we saw death invade more intensely with each passing day. We tried to hold on to hope as we saw him fight for life with a depth of integrity and passion I long to know. Yet we knew we were losing a son, a brother, an uncle, a saint. He would be with us no more. What can you hope for when you are faced with a terminal diagnosis?

I think people can recognize when a battle has been lost. Chuck and I experienced this in the cancer ward with the physical demise of our brother, but we've also seen it many times in the counseling room. A physical cancer often brings a heart to the abyss of despair in the same way a difficult marriage can produce an emotional and spiritual death in the heart. The cancer of the heart is not the pain of loneliness and hurt as much as it is the strident energies of "bitterness, hot tempers, anger, loud quarreling, cursing, and hatred" (Ephesians 4:31, GW). Sadly, many hearts become cancerous and lose the joy of life when conquered by a difficult marriage. We want to affirm what many know but few acknowledge: Pain in a difficult marriage can be agonizing. The truth be told, sometimes the pain of death is more manageable than the perpetual shredding of a heart in a destructive marriage. But in order to thrive, the battle you must fight involves keeping the pain from turning into a ravenous cancer that destroys your heart and stops you from loving well.

Our passion as marriage counselors is to communicate to those in a difficult marriage that while it may feel like it, you are not in the cancer ward. The vacant eyes associated with despair can be filled with life. The frail shoulders now communicating that strength has been depleted can someday exude power. And the bitter voice can lose its cynical tone and begin to laugh again. Life is not over if your marriage feels like a death from a horrible disease. You will not have terminal cancer if you choose to thrive despite your pain. Joy is possible. Our brother Mark taught us this. Even when life was stolen from his body, his heart thrived in ways that caused him to rise above his pain. God refined him in the fire. What the Enemy could never take from him was hope. While he always wished for physical healing, he discovered hope in a good God that transcended his need for a cure from cancer. His hope in a powerful, loving God, who would give him courage to face his pain and offer a promise that all was well despite cancer, resulted in a transformed heart and a joy that could be seen in his penetrating eyes, the windows of his ecstatic soul. The Enemy had lost the battle. As Scripture tells us, "The thief comes only to steal and kill and destroy. I have come that they may have life and have it abundantly" (John 10:10).

DAVE AND PATTY

"You are our last hope. We're going to give this one more try. If you can't fix us, we're going to divorce." Dave and Patty sat grimly across from me (Mike) on my well-worn red couch. The tension in the room revealed the pain the couple carried in their hearts. They were longing for relief from the agony of a marriage that continually wounded their souls and offered no hope for the future.

I began the session addressing them honestly, "Dave and Patty, you've been to counseling before, and you're in a good church, yet nothing has helped. Let me ask both of you, what would make a difference so that you could have hope that your marriage would change for the better?"

"I don't have much hope," Patty said. "I'm willing to change, but he isn't. I know that if he would stop being so angry, life would be a whole lot better. He just hates the world—and me. Nothing I do pleases him. I've tried to tell him how hard it is to live with him, but he just doesn't get it. He only cares about himself."

"You're always blaming me, like you're the great Christian woman, and I'm nothing. I've made lots of changes and what do I get for it? You know, just once I'd like to come home from work and think you were really happy to see me. Just once! If you'd act like a wife for a change and not be so cold and judgmental—don't look at me like that, you know what I mean. If you weren't such an ice princess, maybe I wouldn't be so angry! Whatever . . ."

A thousand thoughts ran through my mind. They needed to learn how to talk constructively. A book on forgiveness would be helpful. Individual counseling for anger management might work. I wondered if they ever prayed together. Did they know how to lighten up and just have fun as a couple? Perhaps sexual abuse was in her background. Does he have a drinking problem? Had they ever had good biblical teaching on the roles a husband and wife assume in marriage? Demon oppression? Do they understand their needs, fears, selfishness, and desires? How about that intensive marital retreat I just read about? Books, seminars, Scripture, and CD series were retrieved from the library of my mind. All good, all helpful. But I went a different route.

I wondered if any of these strategies would help Patty and Dave turn from their destructive patterns and find joy in their marriage. Patty's and Dave's energies were focused on blaming each other for their problems. How could I help them if their marriage remained difficult and a source of ongoing pain? I reviewed two paths often followed when dealing with a difficult marriage. Neither the "Happily Ever After" nor the "Noble Misery" path showed a way to find contentment and joy when having to live in a painful, difficult marriage. I then wondered if God had a way to help people thrive despite facing a future in a troubling marriage. As I continued to ask this question and worked with Chuck and other mature counselors and friends, the "Thriving Despite" path became clear. Let's discuss the first two paths and then take a look at a new path, "Thriving Despite."

Happily Ever After

We have three options for dealing with struggling marriages in the church. The first is to work hard to have a winning marriage by following the "Happily Ever After" model. Some suggest that every marriage can be fixed and filled with deep satisfaction by finding the right principles or skills, or what could be called the "engineering" of relationship. The myth is that a positive, permanent resolution is available for all problems by finding the right engineering. In a success-oriented, can-do, technological society, we often reduce complex problems into a list of right and wrong behaviors and attitudes. This list is made into a series of practical steps which, if followed correctly, will resolve the problems. We see these as the "how to's," or the engineering of living. Nowhere is this more true than in our understanding of how good marriages work. But finding and committing to the right engineering cannot guarantee a great marriage. Be cautious of writers and speakers who are "marriage motivators" and guarantee success for those who apply their revolutionary tools.

The truth is most couples can enrich their marriages by working hard on them and developing strong relational skills. The Christian community has countless resources for troubled marriages or good marriages in which the couple wants to get better. In our counseling practice we are continually searching for the best techniques to help troubled couples. Thankfully, many of these techniques and skills have improved marriages dramatically. We love to tell and hear stories of couples who have turned their marriages around by learning each other's love language, learning to control their negative emotions, or deepening an understanding of each other's needs. We see couples holding hands in church and smiling because all is well. But those whose marriages remain difficult kick themselves (or their spouses) and sink into despair when they see these happy couples. The "Happily Ever After" model has some significant problems.

First, while everyone desires to be happy, this is not a biblical purpose for marriage. Marriage can hold times of great happiness, but God does not promise a lifetime of ongoing happiness. What he does promise is a life of peace, contentment, joy, fulfillment, and many other things—but not perpetual happiness. Should we seek happiness if we have a terminally ill child? Though we may be joyful or content, can you see that the desire for happiness doesn't fit the situation? We are waiting to be convinced that Christ was happy on the road to Gethsemane. He experienced many emotions as he loved in the most profound way imaginable, but it's doubtful he was happy. The idea that happiness is the greatest good and is the ultimate measure of well-being is a completely secular concept and demonstrates a profound misunderstanding of God's intention for life this side of eternity.

Second, some people never take responsibility for their behavior. They make their spouses pay for a lifetime of unhappiness. There is great power in the role of a victim, and some spouses will use their role as *victim* as a way of life. Blame shifting, denial, distortion, lying, and rationalization are some of the ways responsibility is avoided. We are all selfish and self-seeking. Many spouses who feel unjustly treated simply are hardened and not accessible. They will never look at their part in the marital difficulties. If both people do not take responsibility for their part of the problems in their marriage, full intimacy and healing are not possible.

Third, some people are not easy to live with. Many spouses are unpleasant and not likely to change. Difficult spouses range from "good but flawed" to "evil and destructive." For example, living with a physically or emotionally ill spouse is hard. Marriage to a hateful person who continually tries to put you down is like trying to survive on the battlefield while having no gun. Insisting one should have a happily-ever-after marriage with a difficult spouse is like expecting rotting food to be able to nourish your body.

Noble Misery

The second choice we have for surviving in a difficult marriage is to live in "Noble Misery" and suffer ongoing wretchedness since divorce is not an option. You must minimize complaining and do your best to survive the mess you've committed your lives to. Many people reading this book live in painful marriages that hold little to no promise for healing. For reasons of commitment, children, or finances, divorce is not viewed as an alternative. When you are faced with the reality of living with a spouse who has caused or is causing enormous pain, you may not only experience despair—you may be on the road to clinical depression. The martyr or perpetual victim trudges on with nobility and brokenness of spirit. Consigned to a life of misery, the suffering spouse prays for the strength to endure. While we have the greatest compassion for someone in this situation, the "Noble Misery" model has several flaws.

First, no one has to live as a victim. As we will see, living as a victim can be destructive to self and others. You can choose to draw your energy from your pain or from the hope that God places in you. Life is possible even if you have been harmed or wounded in your marriage. Even someone who has truly been victimized has a choice to not live as a victim.

Second, a spouse cannot be your only hope for a meaningful existence. If this is true, then your spouse has become an idol and not a spouse. Living as a defeated person in noble misery keeps you tied to your spouse as your only hope. While a good marriage can provide much joy, God offers life with meaningful satisfaction in many areas other than marriage. Learning to respond to marital difficulties with strength and courage can provide satisfaction even if your spouse will not embrace your love. Refusing to thrive because your spouse and marriage remain difficult is laziness and irresponsibility.

Third, it is possible to thrive while sorrowful. A difficult marriage causes sorrow, but the sorrow doesn't need to be terminal. Jesus was a man of sorrows and was acquainted with grief, but that didn't stop him from moving ahead with his life of great passion. It is possible to live in paradox: being ever sorrowful yet filled with joy (see 2 Corinthians 4:8).

Thriving Despite

Let's consider a third model for people who find themselves in difficult marriages: a commitment to being alive and passionate in a marriage that has ongoing difficulties. We'll call it the "Thriving Despite" model. In other words, *I've got one life to live, and I will live it well no matter what trouble comes my way.* While every attempt should be made to heal a troubled marriage, the lack of a smooth-running marriage should not stop a person from engaging in life. Many people have never considered that life can be satisfying even if their marriage is difficult. We suggest that if a person commits to thriving despite marital troubles, he or she will be in the best position to not only live life well but also offer healthy resources toward their marriage and family. As we begin to discuss the "Thriving Despite" model, let us put a few precautions in place.

First, we are not saying people can't change and therefore you should give up on your marriage. Never, ever give up hope. Marriage demands that we work hard. Go to counseling, study the Word, read books, pray, attend classes, and go on weekend retreats. If you can find something to improve your marriage, utilize it. But don't put your life on hold until your marriage is healed or until your spouse gets it and changes in the way you desire. We *are* saying that some people don't significantly change. If you are married to such a person, your life's ambition can't be to get your spouse to change. If you put your life on hold waiting for your spouse to change, you may wake up one morning and realize you have wasted your life.

Next, we are also not saying that you should just forget about your spouse and focus on your own self-fulfillment. This is not a book about justifying selfishness. In reality, by accepting your spouse and not demanding change, you will be free to love from a stronger, healthier, more godly perspective. When your perspective changes from looking for a change in your spouse to strengthening your own heart, you'll be able to offer a love that is hard to dismiss.

With this method we are not promoting the "Parallel Path" model of marriage. In the "Parallel Path" model, which many in the "Noble Misery" model end up following, difficult marriages are managed by spouses choosing to learn to coexist in peace while they seek their deepest life satisfaction outside of marriage. They basically remain closed to each other and give up all hope of finding meaning and joy in their relationship. Though pulling away from the destructive dynamics a difficult spouse presents is important to thriving, quitting on the marriage is not what we are suggesting. We're saying that the path of thriving frees a person to no longer require marriage or the spouse to heal his or her wounds and provide ongoing life satisfaction.

THE THREE ROADS FOR A DIFFICULT MARRIAGE

HAPPILY EVER AFTER	NOBLE MISERY	THRIVING DESPITE
Happily ever after	The unsuccessful marriage	The well-lived life
My spouse will change	My spouse won't change	I accept my spouse may not change
My marriage will be blissful	My marriage is miserable	My marriage may remain difficult
I will be happy	I will always be unhappy	I have joy
My future will be happy	My future is to grin and bear it	I have a rich future
My kids will have a great family	My kids will survive	I can provide hope for my kids
God is blessed by me	God suffers with me	God can delight in me
My marriage and I are a success	My marriage and I are a failure	I am imperfect but offering my best
I am happy to go on	I have no choice but to go on	I will go on and thrive, despite
The goal is happiness	The goal is just to survive	The goal is to thrive and live well

THE NEED FOR WISDOM

As we've discussed these ideas about thriving in a difficult marriage with friends and clients, they invariably say, "I like the idea, but how do you do this? What are the steps? (What's the engineering?)"

While being practical is a good thing, beginning to practice the "Thriving Despite" model requires a shift of thinking. *The key to thriving despite a difficult marriage is developing wisdom.* Wisdom doesn't require that we master a set of technical skills but rather that we enter a path guided by exercising core convictions. These convictions include:

1. *Marriage means partnering with God.* Holding a belief that God is in it.

He loves you and your spouse and is molding and shaping you. When we stand before a holy God and commit our lives to another, we become involved in a threesome. God is intensely involved in our marriage, whether it's an easy or trying one. From the backyard to the bedroom, God is there. His heart desires good things for us. Yet we must understand that marriage is one of the prime ways he will shape our character. If you will commune with God, he will show you your passions and your selfishness as they are played out with your spouse. You'll be challenged to love and grieve with an energy and wisdom that can be drawn only from his resources. He will not abandon you in your marital struggles. You are not journeying alone. Your pain is not without purpose. Thriving will not be possible unless God is working through you.

2. *Marriage is bigger than you.* Maintaining a conviction that marriage is worth giving yourself to no matter the cost.

You marry and invest in someone you believe is most likely to bring you meaningful life satisfaction. It is the rare person who understands that marriage is greater than the two individuals who have vowed to remain together for a lifetime. Marriage has a meaning and purpose far beyond personal happiness and the need for satisfaction. In the same way you're not in your marriage simply to have your needs met, you don't remain in your marriage just to keep your vow or commitment. A belief in marriage means that you are willing to yield yourself to the requirements your marriage presents you. In a difficult marriage that may mean that you learn how to love and endure when you receive little in return.

3. *Marriage requires honesty.* Possessing a willingness to relentlessly pursue truth about yourself, your spouse, and the state of your marriage.

You need to know yourself, who you are, what you've done, and what you want. You also need to know your spouse in the same way. We are masters at believing what we want to believe and choosing to deny the truth. The human denial and distortion system is one of the great mysteries of our being. A person can be a raging alcoholic and yet really believe he or she has his or her drinking totally under control. One has only to watch a reality show like *American Idol* to recognize that few people have an accurate view of themselves. Even the most off-pitch, unmusical singer believes he or she is the greatest talent in the country—despite direct feedback to the contrary. Few people are able to correct wrong self-perceptions even when given accurate evaluations by others.

Only when people earnestly desire to know the truth about who they are and who they are married to can they begin to deal honestly with the struggles in their marriages. A willingness to continually pursue an authentic awareness of the good, bad, ugly, and beautiful about yourself and your spouse will eventually shatter the denial and distortion system and lead to a refreshing freedom that only honesty can bring. Part of knowing the truth includes having knowledge of what you can and cannot do. You can't change your spouse. You are not responsible for your spouse's behavior or attitudes. However, you can take responsibility for your response to your spouse. The ability to respond to difficulty from your godly, redeemed nature as opposed to your selfish, corrupt nature is something you can do with God's help.

4. *The battle is in the heart.* Having a passion to maintain integrity of heart and keep hope alive.

We suggest that the real struggle in marriage is in the heart. Our Enemy will attack our hearts so they become devoid of love and passion. Your commitment must be to never allow that to happen, no matter what troubles your marriage may bring to you. Paul understood this struggle accurately when he explained in 1 Corinthians 13 that performance and behavior, even of the most sacrificial nature, are meaningless if they are driven by a heart without love. You are on the right path when you understand that the true problem that needs to be addressed doesn't concern the defects in your spouse but rather the darkness that emerges from your own heart while in a difficult marriage. Change can occur when you look in the mirror and say that you don't like what you see. You find your heart becoming hateful, weak, disrespectful, or numb. The path of wisdom dictates that you must repent of the directions your heart has taken as opposed to justifying them because you have a tough marriage.

Hope

This third model of marriage has a unique understanding of hope. The hope in the "Happily Ever After" marriage is for personal fulfillment and pleasant circumstances. In the "Noble Misery" model the hope is that God will provide enough strength to survive the mess. In the "Thriving Despite" model, the concept of hope looks like this:

> Your hope is that God will give you the wisdom, courage, and strength to defeat the Enemy's attempts to corrupt your heart so you can remain alive and passionate. With a thriving heart you will be able to live vibrantly and allow God to offer a powerful love through you to whomever he puts in your path, especially your spouse. The result is that God will be honored and life will be immensely fulfilling.

The goal of this book is not to offer another strategy to get your spouse's attention or to find the way to successfully heal your marriage. But someone who commits to thriving despite will be in the best position to have a strong marriage. A thriving person is willing to accept who the spouse really is without an agenda to change the partner. Thriving people are prepared to accept that certain things may never happen in their marriage and to grieve the loss. For example, they may never have a spouse they can truly trust or be with a mate who pursues them passionately. By accepting and grieving the loss of things that will not happen (what is *not* possible), a person becomes free to focus on what *is* possible in the marriage. For example, you may find yourself thinking, *Okay, you will never be a great spiritual leader or encourager of dreams, but I will discover something in you that is valuable and we can enjoy, even if it's only in passing moments.*

HOPE FOR PATTY AND DAVE

"You both are saying that your hope for a better marriage is dependent on the other person changing. My guess is that you are experts in telling each other how badly you are being failed. I'm sure you have communicated countless ways the other could change so that you could be happier. And you're sitting here hoping that I can get your message across to your spouse so you can get some relief. I want to challenge you to consider another way. Dave, what if Patty never changes into a woman who enjoys sex with you or appreciates you as a man? Patty, what if Dave stays angry and negative and doesn't value your needs?" The feeling of tension in the room changed to the sound of groaning.

"Look, you've spent years being angry and hurt. You are so tired of being in pain. You've tried everything to fix this marriage—mainly to get each other's attention about how the other person is messing up. You are enslaved by your hurts and hopelessness. Neither of you is free to love—your hearts have become corrupt. Would you consider that you can be alive and enjoy life only after you stop trying to survive and fix each other?"

What If:

You believed God was less concerned with whether or not your needs were being met and more concerned with the state of your heart?

You were able to give up all efforts to become happy by trying to change your spouse?

You no longer desired to show your spouse how poorly you are being loved?

You had the capacity to accept your spouse as he or she is and have a lifestyle of forgiveness?

You knew God's grace in a way that freed you from guilt and shame so you could honestly explore the ways you don't love well?

You believed in God's love for you so deeply that you were confident you could love strongly and wisely no matter what?

You committed to finding purpose and passion for life that didn't depend on your spouse's response or approval?

Your heart was no longer characterized by bitterness, despair, pride, or apathy?

You were able to disengage from the destructiveness of your marriage while developing a desire to constructively engage in what was God-honoring?

The look in Patty and Dave's eyes told me they had never considered really being alive and thriving if their spouse never changed. Yet the idea captured something in their souls: There is another way. Hope is alive.

Chapter 2

Why Marriages Are Difficult

"He has hurt me in so many ways. There is nothing inside me that ever wants to go back into that pain. Even if I wanted to, I don't think I could. Something within me has been bound up and is longing to be expressed as a wife, and it never will be as long as I am married to him. Will I ever be able to make sense of all of this?"

Confusion

Patty was crying out for help and looking for hope, but the only thing that was clear to her was that she was in massive pain and desperate for relief. An accumulation of teachings from seminars, books, sermons, and counselors made her feel that whatever she was thinking was probably wrong. She knew she didn't want to hate Dave, but she was no longer willing to forgive him just because he had a tough childhood. Her pastor's advice was to trust God, forgive Dave, practice loving behaviors and attitudes, and then believe that loving feelings would follow her actions. It sounded so good, so right. Yet, after talking with her pastor why did she feel like her problems had been trivialized? As she walked out of his office, she felt defeated and convinced that no one had the remotest idea of the depth of the torment and confusion in her soul. She was alone and without hope.

People struggling in difficult marriages are often confused about what they are feeling and thinking. In the counseling room Chuck and I are often asked questions such as, "Should I feel guilty for thinking that my wife is cold and uncaring?" or "What am I supposed to feel when he yells at me?" Often they ask, "What's the 'right' way to think or feel about what's going on in my marriage?"

Patty struggled to make sense of the confusing thoughts and emotions she felt about Dave. *It feels wrong to be bitter. But I was never bitter before,* she thought, *so Dave must be the cause. Yet some of the things he wants from me seem reasonable, so maybe he was right to criticize me the way he did. I really haven't been very warm to him. What if he is right to be so upset with me? But he swore at me when I was too tired last night. A godly husband never swears at his wife when she's too tired for sex! So I should be allowed to be upset with him.*

Voices come at strugglers from every possible angle, offering opinions on why their marriage is in trouble and offering unsolicited solutions: "Stop complaining and submit. If you would just trust God, your spouse would . . ." "Perhaps he's not as bad as you think." "Maybe she's right that you are selfish." "Once an abuser, always an abuser—you'd better leave him!" "I told you that you shouldn't marry him! You knew he wasn't really a believer!" "What did you expect when she comes from a family like that?"

In trying to untangle the web of confusion in a difficult marriage, discouragement and defeat may exhaust the strongest of hearts and frustrate the best of intentions. It is important to find a way to get to the core issues in order to remove confusion. What is really going on? In order to bring order to the chaos of a difficult marriage and develop a plan to thrive, you need to know what's causing the difficulties. What is the problem?

What's Wrong with My Marriage?

Is your marriage difficult and causing you pain because you have communication problems and fight all the time? Are things not working because you don't spend enough time together? Is the basic problem in your marriage that your spouse had an affair or looks at pornography, or is it that she doesn't ever forget anything wrong you have ever done? Or do you think you lack a common vision and fail to support each other in your dreams? Is it a lack of forgiveness or prayer? Or is it conflict with in-laws?

There is an easy answer: *The problem is your spouse!* He or she is an insensitive, selfish, controlling person. Nothing you can do will ever make him or her happy. He or she doesn't treat you the way you want to be treated. He or she doesn't understand your needs. He or she doesn't hear you. He or she doesn't _respect me_ (you fill in the blank). And you're probably right: He or she isn't doing what would make your marriage work for *you*. Your spouse is the problem. It's what you live with every day. You wake up with it, and you go to sleep with it. No one has to tell you what the problem is; you already know. If my spouse would only change, do this or that, the marriage would be great. He or she is at fault. He or she doesn't love me the way a spouse should.

There are many ways to define marital problems and diagnose difficulties in marriage. Every psychologist who counsels couples is presented with a myriad of problem areas in a marriage. Depending on his theoretical orientation, experience, and wisdom, he will choose a problem area that promises to yield the most satisfying result. It could be communication skills, understanding differences in needs, relational dynamics, biblical roles, and more. Yet in their core almost all couples believe the difficulties in their marriages are caused by their spouses. But if you focus on your spouse's defects you will only become more self-righteous and miserable. What you choose to see as the central issue in your troubled marriage will determine whether you flounder or thrive. Hint: the problem isn't your spouse. It's something else.

Moving to the Inside

Chuck and I too have chosen to focus on a specific area. As we have studied, prayed, and groaned with couples seeking help, we've developed a perspective on what the key issue is in a difficult marriage. By defining the problem in a specific way, we will take you on a journey to deepen your understanding of the problem and develop a plan to help you thrive despite your ongoing marital problems.

Simply put:

- Your spouse does not offer what you long to receive.
- He or she does not ask of you what you desire to give.
- Consequently, you suffer the pain of disappointment.

Your basic problem is:

- You have difficulty keeping your heart alive and good in the face of ongoing, painful disappointment.

Don't let the simplicity of this statement prevent you from exploring the depth of its meaning. When Jesus said he came to save the lost, he was saying that our basic dilemma wasn't an inability to solve the practical problems of living. Instead, he came to deal with an internal, abstract issue: the corruption in our hearts. When God told Samuel how to select the next king among Jesse's sons, God told him "The Lord sees not as man sees: man looks on the outward appearance, but the Lord looks on the heart" (1 Samuel 16:7). The heart is the source of our thirst and where our deepest problems lie.

In order to grasp the difficulties you have as you face disappointment in marriage, you will need to understand the power and importance of the desires of your heart. Desire is provoked and exposed by disappointment. You will discover that beneath all pain and disappointment desire is crying out for satisfaction. When God is drawing us to himself, he often uses pain in our lives to stimulate a thirst in our hearts for relationship with him. In tough times we turn to God when we become aware that life is not offering us what we long to receive, nor is anyone asking what we long to give (our love, gifts, talents). We become disappointed and bring our dissatisfaction to God, asking him to provide satisfaction for our desires.

What you will discover throughout this book is that you are not clear about what you desire nor is it likely you handle disappointment well. The interplay between desire and disappointment leads to corruption in the heart. This corruption needs to be understood and clarified, with God's grace, so that healthy desires can be embraced and the heart can be kept alive and thriving despite disappointment.

Desire and Disappointment — Three Reasons You Are Having Marital Problems

1. You are not offered what you long to receive, but you are offered what you don't want to receive.
2. You are not asked for what you long to give, but you are asked for what you don't want to give.
3. You have difficulty keeping your heart alive and good in the face of ongoing disappointed desires.

Let's take a deeper look at the first reason:

You are not offered what you long to receive.

Eddie remembered how his mother used to speak about his father. She would tell him and anyone else she talked to that her husband was a hardworking man who had given up a lot to take care of the needs of his family. It was clear to Eddie that his mom appreciated his dad, affirming him and admiring who he was as a man. When he got married to Rachael, he assumed that she would view him in much the same way.

In Rachael's home, however, her father wasn't held in high esteem. A man who had gone from job to job, more interested in playing around than working hard, he hadn't earned the respect of her mother, who was free with her criticism and contempt. Rachael adopted her mother's attitude toward her dad.

After twenty years of marriage, Eddie finally accepted that what he longed to receive would never happen. "Dad" would never be celebrated in his home, and the deep respect and admiration he longed for from his wife would never happen. Rather than rich fulfillment of his heart's desire, he experienced the pains of rejection. He desired to be respected as a man and husband, something Rachael was unwilling or unable to offer. He would never know the love of an appreciative wife.

You look to your spouse as a source of life who is equipped to understand and fulfill your desires. When you ask to be loved and respected, you want your spouse to offer to give you what you long for so you can experience satisfaction. When your spouse does not give you what you have requested, you are unfulfilled and disappointed. Since you believe that what your heart craves can be found in your marriage, you are hurt and troubled when your desire isn't fulfilled. When you are not offered what you long to receive, you feel emptiness, pain, or dissatisfaction.

But you are offered what you don't want to receive.

Rachael related to Eddie much the way her mother related to her father. Nothing he ever did was good enough for her. If he took her out to a restaurant, it was the wrong restaurant. If he bought her jewelry, it wasn't the right style. And when he tried a home-repair project, all she noticed were the imperfections.

What Rachael offered him was a wife who would criticize and demean his efforts to be a husband and leader of the home. While his soul was designed to be respected, he was offered disrespect and contempt. His heart had to deal with ongoing assaults with no relief. Eddie felt like he was in a boxing match with a fighter who kept knocking him down and the bell to end the round never rang. His marriage was a joyless battle to survive unremitting disdain and contempt from his wife.

You have an idea of what you want from your marriage and your spouse. When, instead of getting what you thought you were going to get, you are offered something different, something you don't want, you have a problem. You, as the husband in our example, feel like you are being assaulted with criticism and disrespect. Instead of hearing about how your wife appreciates all you do for her, you are being offered criticism, negativity, and challenges to do even more for your family. Rather than being given praise as a hero, you are receiving condemnation. Your desires are disappointed and you now have to cope with a wounded heart.

Most people in a troubled marriage are offered what they don't want to receive. If you believed you were getting a responsible spouse, and your spouse is irresponsible, you are not only disappointed but you have to cope with his or her irresponsibility. If, instead of getting a spouse who is filled with integrity, you have a spouse who has little integrity, you are getting what you don't want. Instead of getting a spouse who is a sports fanatic, you got one who loves antiques, or if you thought you would have a spouse who would give you a lot of space, but instead you got a spouse who won't let you breathe, you have a problem because you have to contend with what you don't want. More important, you are left with a disappointed heart.

You are not asked for what you long to give.

Ann knew Tim was troubled when she married him. He had been kicked around by life and wrestled with depression and self-confidence. But she knew he had a good heart, loved the Lord, and was a gifted man. She wanted to offer her strength and care to help him become all he was designed to be. Wisdom, tenderness, and feminine strength were but a few of the gifts she longed to share with him.

On their fifteenth anniversary, she wept alone in her bed. Tim was gone on another business trip, one conveniently arranged to avoid having to be with her on their anniversary. She was coming into an inescapable realization that Tim was a loner and didn't want anything from anyone, especially her. Nothing she offered him was received. If she wanted to give him her time, she was told she was smothering him. When she gave him input on how he might connect better with the kids, he told her she had a critical spirit. And when she offered him affection, he didn't want anything that was "long and involved." Her ideas about what he could do in his career were seen as intrusive and controlling. Tim told her that her desire to have more children with him was selfish and stupid. Ann ached with the realization that so much of what God had designed for her to offer her husband would never be asked for by Tim.

Most people in a difficult marriage are not asked for what they long to give. You want to give your strength and leadership to your spouse, and she isn't interested in that at all. You want to give your nurturing and tenderness to your spouse, and he couldn't care less. You want to invite your spouse into your dreams and hopes, and your spouse doesn't know what you are talking about when you share your ideas for the future. There is much about you as a man or woman you would love to share with your spouse, but when you do, you are met with rejection. As a result, you must cope with not being asked for what you desire to give. You are left to experience the pain of loneliness and lack of fulfillment. You feel stagnated and only half alive. You must learn to cope with a spouse who doesn't want what you desire to give.

But you are asked for what you don't want to give.
Tim was absorbed in his career. He could be appreciated there without ever having to get close to people. The home and family were left to Ann. What Tim wanted from her was a domestic business manager, governess, sex partner, and sounding board. Ann never wanted to be a person who had to take responsibility for the bills, home repair and maintenance, as well as the spiritual and social life of the family. With all Tim required of her, her stress level was through the roof. And, oh

yes, he did want sex with her. He needed stress relief. He also wanted her to feel sorry for how difficult his road life was and how he never could get a break. Ann was married to a man who kept asking of her what she never wanted to give. She never wanted to be a distant partner who was stuck with all the responsibility with no hope of ever being loved and cherished, much less appreciated. Having to feel sorry for a little boy (Tim) was not what she wanted to offer a husband, but that was all that he asked of her. Her future was one filled with the agony of having to give what she didn't want to offer while never being asked for what she really longed to provide.

Many difficulties in marriage occur when someone is asked for what he or she never wanted to give. Your spouse wants you to talk a lot, and you don't like to talk. She wants you to be more emotional, so you struggle to express emotions that don't exist. Your spouse insists on sex far more often than you would like, and you are asked to offer your body when you have no desire. You are asked to give your body, emotions, time, and energies in ways you don't really want to. You don't always think what is being asked of you is good, but you feel like you have to give it anyway. You are in pain because you are exhausted and don't even know who you are anymore. You've tried to become who your spouse wants you to be, but you've done so at a great price. Your marriage is difficult because it asks you to give what you don't want to give while not asking for what you want to give.

Our third and most significant reason for marital problems is this:

You have difficulty keeping your heart alive and good in the face of ongoing disappointed desires.
As you've read the examples of Eddie and Rachael and Tim and Ann, perhaps you are thinking they simply need to understand each other better. They seem to have a radically different understanding of one another's needs and agendas. If they could only see from each other's points of view, the problems could be cleared up. We agree. But as we will discuss throughout this book, *many difficult marriages have one or*

both spouses who will never be able to see life from any perspective but his or her own. By spending years trying to change your spouse's perspective, you may never face the one problem God can help you with—**your own disappointment.** This is the key issue. Can you begin to think that the pain you are experiencing is a response to the fact that you are not getting what you desire? The challenge you have is finding a way to keep your heart good and alive in the face of ongoing pain. If you begin to explore this simple truth, you may discover a way through the hopelessness of your marriage. The place to begin to face your pain is to develop a confidence that you understand what you are offering and asking of your spouse. The pain and turmoil of marital conflict can cause great confusion, so it's important to clarify the agendas of the heart.

CLARIFYING

Definition: To make desires clear by exposing and removing distortions and confusion. The result is a pure and powerful expression of the longings of the heart.

The amount of confusion that exists in a difficult marriage cannot be overstated. In order to thrive, an individual must clarify understanding to minimize confusion and bring about the truth about the condition of his or her marriage. Then the heart can be better seen. Hope cannot be found in confusion. In the story of Patty and Dave you may understand that Patty's confidence in her ability to see her marriage clearly seemed to change with the day of the week, the week of her cycle, or the phases of the moon. Some days she was certain Dave was a monster and her anger felt justified, while other days she would wake up thinking she was just having a pity party and needed to trust God more.

So because of confusion, many people are unclear about what it is they long to offer and receive. As a result, they are unable to address the issues of a disappointed heart. Focusing on two critical questions will reduce confusion and help you address the third question on how to keep your heart alive through disappointment. As you ask these questions, you will have a way to organize your thinking so you can develop a plan to thrive despite a difficult marriage. The three critical questions are:

1. Do you know what you want to receive and offer?
2. Do you know if what you want is good?
3. Do you know how to keep your heart alive and good when you are disappointed?

As you wrestle with these three questions, you will begin to understand the problems you must address in order to thrive in your difficult marriage. The answer to the first question, "Do you know what you want to receive and offer?" is not nearly as obvious as you might think. Most people do not know what it is they are really looking for in their spouse or what their spouse is looking for in them. Few people understand the importance of our desires, that they drive all we do.

The second question, "Do you know if what you want is good and healthy, as opposed to bad and unhealthy?" is also not easy to answer. Most people assume that what they want is healthy and good, and rarely stop to question if what they want is good or bad. How can you know? Most people who are in pain assume that the problem is they didn't get the good thing they wanted. They don't entertain the possibility that they were refused what they wanted because it wasn't a good thing. How many husbands have thought that wanting their wives to give them unquestioning obedience was a good desire when it was actually a selfish one? How many wives have thought that wanting their husbands to always defer to them as a queen was a healthy desire instead of an unhealthy one?

While you hope for a mutually enhancing love, your history of interacting with a fallen world has affected your understanding and experience of your desires. *Do I want too much, too little? Is what my spouse is asking of me good for our marriage?* You may be confused that your spouse has not treated you the way you hoped, and it has never crossed your mind that what you've been expecting from your spouse and your marriage may not be good. Because of a lack of understanding of what God has intended for your marriage and as a result of confusion from relationships in your past, you may be in pain because you have wanted unhealthy things without knowing it. The pain you feel doesn't tell you whether or not what you want is good or bad. You may be in pain because you were denied a good thing or in pain because you were denied a bad thing. You must clarify and understand what it is you desire before you can thrive.

Symbiosis: Wanting Yourself, Not a Beloved

Another reason it is difficult to know if our desires are good is that we are all self-centered by nature. We think, feel, and behave in response to our own needs. It is natural. No one scratches an itch because someone tells them they should. The awareness comes from self. The problem is we instinctually think people should be like us and have the same itch. Liberals think people should think like a liberal. Conservatives think everyone should think like a conservative. New Yorkers think they have the right view on life while Midwesterners believe their way of seeing life is better than that of either coast. The truth is, no two people share the same fingerprints, and no two people see the world in exactly the same way. Different perspectives challenge our way of seeing life, and we don't like them, especially when someone else's way causes us to have to adjust. Just try to change the style of music in your church if you doubt what we are saying.

When we get married something within us instinctually desires to shape our spouse into our own image. Harvel Hendrix and Helen Hunt call this "symbiosis."[1] Without giving it much thought we have symbiotic fantasies that our spouse will learn to like the things we like, start to think the way we do, and generally be in sync with our way of living. But the reality is that "sameness" is a myth. If God had wanted husbands and wives to be alike, he would've created them to be the same. God in his great wisdom did not do this. While male and female are created in God's image and are equal, he created them with wonderful distinctives. God's creativity and sense of humor play out in the way he designed the sexual differences between men and women. Men and women experience sex in entirely different ways and often play out a comedy of errors trying to find a way to mutually satisfy each other.

In a healthy marriage, a husband and wife enjoy the differences in each other, strive to enhance them and combine with them to become complete. In a difficult marriage, the dissimilarities cause significant obstacles to harmony, and rather than moving a couple toward oneness, they cause division. Difficult spouses often do not tolerate differences well. They insist on sameness and are bewildered or angered when their husband or wife doesn't want what they want or agree with their view. Your spouse may never accept that you see your marriage differently and as a result, he or she will go to war with you over the differences. Many partners only allow one voice or opinion in their marriage: his or her own voice.

WISDOM

One aspect of wisdom is to understand that God is partnering with you in your marriage. In order to determine if what you want is good, you must ask if what you want furthers God's purposes for your marriage. This is not always easy to do because we are masters at justifying our own agendas by saying they are God's agendas.

Let's look at the man who says his desire for his wife to be obedient to him is good because the Bible teaches that a woman should submit to her husband and obey him. He may get a scriptural reference to back up his point. He uses the Bible to develop technical procedures his wife should follow in order to guarantee a godly marriage and satisfaction for him.

Wisdom requires that the man know his own heart, that he is capable of having a selfish agenda. It also calls him to understand God's principles, not as specific rules to follow in order to please a strict, authoritarian God, but as pathways leading to the joy of relationship with God and with his wife. If he does not understand his wife as his equal, he may use his desire to try to diminish and master her. He wants her to obey him for his own — not God's — purposes. But if he realizes that his wife bears God's image just as he does, then he desires she offer strength under his leadership, not to serve him, but so the harmony and mutual respect in their marriage would develop into a force that celebrates God.

The third question, "Do you know how to keep your heart alive and good when you are disappointed?" is one that we will help you explore throughout this book. While it is instinctual to think your spouse is the problem because he or she doesn't give you what you want, an understanding of your own reaction and response to disappointment is vital to thriving in marriage.

Through clarifying you will discover that your thinking, perspective, and understanding will become refined. Your goal is to reach a place where you can know you are offering an authentic love, rejecting evil, and having an *accurate* attitude of forgiveness, repentance, and a call to holiness. The journey to reach such understanding is long and difficult and requires that you honestly embrace the truth of what is happening in your marriage and your heart. To face the prospect of a marriage with ongoing pain requires courage. While it is inspiring to read stories of courageous people who fought epic battles and overcame significant obstacles, we realize it might be easier to fight the big epic battle than endure the daily, moment-by-moment war that goes on in the soul of someone facing a loveless, difficult marriage.

The Battle for Your Heart — Keeping Your Heart Alive and Good

You may be thinking that your struggle to keep your heart alive and good only involves your spouse. It is not that simple. The real battle is not merely with your spouse; it is also with another enemy, an intruder who is at war not only with you, but also with your Creator. That Enemy has an agenda to rob your soul of the purity and beauty God desires it to display, replacing it with a life-ending cancer. He is a brilliant tactician who knows precisely where to attack and destroy you without being detected. The Enemy targets your heart. The thief who steals its goodness is a spiritual enemy. *His goal is that your heart will become bitter, despairing, proud, or apathetic by living with a difficult spouse.* As a heart becomes darkened or numbed, it loses integrity and the ability to love. When this occurs, the enemy wins because the beauty and the glory God intended for you to celebrate in your marriage is gone.

Paul warns us, "But if you bite and devour one another, watch out that you are not consumed by one another" (Galatians 5:15). The Evil One is brilliant at getting spouses to turn and devour each other. Start shifting from seeing your spouse as the only enemy to viewing Satan as the real opponent. Fighting against the real Enemy in order to keep your heart whole and alive is central to your ability to thrive in the warfare found in an imperfect marriage. If you don't understand this larger battle, your heart will be weak and confused. You must discover the larger battle in order to protect your heart and fight wisely.

Oswald Chambers, in his book on Job, *Baffled to Fight Better*, says it best: "The explanation of Job's suffering is the fact that God and Satan had made a battleground of his soul. He further states, "Everyone's soul represents some kind of battlefield."[2] Satan's strategy was to bring negative circumstances to Job so he would no longer trust in the goodness of God. The Enemy wants to attack your heart so you are in despair. You don't believe you will ever see God's goodness in your difficult marriage. Satan is warring with God and the spiritual battle ground is your soul. The thief wants to steal, kill, and destroy your heart. He is using your marriage to accomplish his goal. Christ is fighting for you and in you. Your and your spouse's hearts are precious to God.

The Enemy knows this and will spare nothing and no one in his attempts to conquer your heart. If he can give you a spiritual cancer by producing despair, bitterness, pride, or apathy, he has won your heart. Satan desires to corrupt you and take ownership of your being. While he can never own God's children, he can declare war to control the energies and well-being of the heart. He does it by tempting you to give in to your pain or shame, to tempt you to turn from God, and to move your heart away from love. But God offers strength through his spirit to fight the most severe battles, those that expose the deepest wounds and most shameful flaws within you. And remember, in the end God wins; Satan loses.

"Yeah, right! You want me to believe that God and Satan are fighting over me? God's got bigger things to do than to fight for territory in my soul. I'm not that important." Whether you think you are important or not isn't the issue. What matters is that God has chosen to involve you and your marriage in the cosmic struggle against evil. He wants you to win. As he did with Job, God has agreed to enter a battle with the Enemy to test and develop the loyalty and strength of men's and women's souls. Because of the spiritual significance of marriage, your union with your mate is where the battle for your heart is the fiercest and is a lifelong campaign. Many people, divorced and married, lose the war. Winning the battle requires that you willingly engage in the fierce fight to retain and strengthen your heart's ability to love well and keep hope alive despite pain. When you shift to this spiritual understanding of what is going on within you, you realize the battle in your hearts is critical and has eternal significance.

For we do not wrestle against flesh and blood, but against the rulers, against the authorities, against the cosmic powers over this present darkness, against the spiritual forces of evil in the heavenly places. (Ephesians 6:12)

As you begin to become conscious of the intense siege against you, you understand that only a passion to maintain integrity energized by the strength God provides will help you survive the battle and keep your heart vital and pure. Yet guarding your heart is a lifelong battle. To fight this battle well will require wrestling with the agony experienced in a painful marriage and seeking God's strength to keep your heart alive and uncorrupted in the face of ongoing difficulty and disappointment.

Hope

The "Thriving Despite" model encourages what is not available in the "Happily Ever After" or "Noble Misery" models for addressing the concerns of difficult marriages. The "Happily Ever After" path insists on the satisfaction of thirsts without the burden of disappointment while the "Noble Misery" approach targets bearing the burden of disappointments without keeping desires strong. With the "Thriving Despite" model you will learn to broaden your heart's capacity to accommodate paradox: an alive heart and a wounded heart, or the ability to embrace both satisfying expressions of desire and the pain felt in disappointment. Paul wrote about this when he wrote, "As sorrowful, yet always rejoicing" (2 Corinthians 6:10).

By focusing on this single issue, you can learn to face the difficulties in your marriage with joy and not fear the times of deep disappointment and sorrow. The Enemy may cause you great pain in your marriage, but he cannot steal the joy of life Christ offers you.

In the next chapter we will explore God's design for healthy desires. We will learn what men and women are designed to ask and offer to each other. God's pattern for healthy hearts will serve as a reference point for you to clarify the desires of your soul.

PART 2

The Heart of a Marriage

DARKNESS AND LIGHT

CHAPTER 3

The Desiring Heart

There is a nagging awareness inside us, warning that we'd better not
feel our hunger too deeply or it will undo us.[1]
— *John Eldredge*

The LORD sees not as man sees: man looks on the outward
appearance, but the LORD looks on the heart.
— *1 Samuel 16:7*

The road map we are going to use to guide you through the clarifying and cleansing process—into the battle for your heart and into a thriving existence—contains four hearts. Understanding each heart separately and how they work together will provide a framework from which you can move forward with hope. The four hearts will be presented sequentially as if you will go from one to the next, but in actuality, parts of you exist in all four hearts simultaneously. By understanding the journey of the heart, an individual will begin to understand how thriving is possible despite living in a difficult marriage.

Simply stated, you have a Desiring Heart that longs for deep, loving connection with your beloved. Your Desiring Heart, filled with passion and hope, engages with the heart of your spouse. In a difficult marriage, it encounters rejection, turmoil, and assault and surfaces as a Wounded Heart. As it attempts to cope with the pain of marital wounds, the

Wounded Heart develops into a Surviving Heart and develops complex strategies for surviving pain and confusion. Finally, freedom is found when survival strategies are recognized as futile, self-centered, and unloving, and repentance occurs. The Thriving Heart emerges from the slavery of trying to survive in a difficult marriage. Godly desires are clarified and expressed, transformation occurs, and the Thriving Heart is able to live and love without requiring that a spouse also change.

As you journey through the four hearts, you will begin to see the redeemed person your spouse could be underneath the flawed person he or she presents to you. But remember, this is a journey of awareness and understanding that leads to action. The journey will go through phases that can't be avoided if real transformation is to be achieved. The idea is to create a hope and a hunger in the heart that moves past pain and resentment and longs for the redemption and wholeness of one's self and spouse. Yet also remember, the goal of this book is not to promote a happily-ever-after marriage or a noble sufferer but to develop the capacity, through Christ, to thrive even if your spouse never responds to your transformed, good heart.

THE HEART

I (Chuck) have had the privilege of visiting a wonderful place at the intersection of Brazil and Argentina—Foz do Iguaçu, where the world's largest waterfalls are located and many Hollywood films have been shot, perhaps most notably *The Mission*. The first time I experienced the magnificence of the expansive falls I was overwhelmed with the beauty, vastness, and power of more than two hundred separate falls stretching between the two countries. I recall standing on a bridge connecting Brazil and Argentina directly across from the falls, speechless and completely awestruck with the scene before me. I spontaneously held both arms up in a ridiculously futile attempt to "take it all in" because there was something within me that desperately wanted to connect with God through this incredible experience. The verse that says "What no eye has seen, nor ear heard, nor the heart of man imagined, what God has prepared for those who love him" (1 Corinthians 2:9) came alive for me.

My desire to connect with my heavenly Father, to somehow comprehend what his world and heaven was all about and the reality of my finiteness—all of this I experienced in a brief moment of time standing there with the water roaring down around me. My desire, my thirst to connect, to be a part of something much larger than me was obvious. I had then, and have now, a difficult time putting that experience into words. But I groaned then and groan now. Words are so inadequate.

We have found that when we talk to clients about their hearts, most people look at us as if they should understand what we are saying, but their vacant stare reveals they are not sure what we mean by "heart." Men tend to dismiss the heart as a soft, feminine notion found only in chick flicks or touchy-feely guys, and not as something important for the average guy. They often want minimal hassle and the conveniences a marriage provides. Some women tend to view the heart sentimentally and emotionally. Others in contemporary culture see the heart as a place where women are weak or vulnerable, so they want only the mechanics of a marriage. Others tell us they know exactly what they want, but the problem is that their husbands aren't giving it to them. If you are to understand how to thrive in a difficult marriage, you must be willing to explore and appreciate the depth and power of your heart.

I recently heard a very good teaching on personal growth that utilized the cognitive approach to change. The speaker emphasized the necessity of training our minds, disciplining our emotions, and realizing we have the ability to choose our own paths. Though I agreed with the general direction of his thought, an essential part of the change process was missing from his talk. He didn't mention the heart. While Scripture often includes thinking capacities when it uses the word *heart*, Jesus differentiated heart, soul, and mind when he said, "You shall love the Lord your God with all your heart and with all your soul and with all your mind" (Matthew 22:37).

When we use the word *heart* in this book, we are talking about the inner being of mankind where motivations, appetites, and affections originate. In Paul's teaching on love in 1 Corinthians 13, he wrote that without love, or a good heart, doing even the most sacrificial act is meaningless. This could be understood to mean that even if I understand the right thing to do—I make good choices, and control my emotions and passions (the engineering of Christianity)—all my good works, choices, and behaviors are meaningless if my heart is not good and pure.

Most of us have been trained in the church to not focus on the heart except as it is expressed in an emotional or sentimental way toward God. Somehow the desires and passions of the heart have been associated with selfishness or sin. It is true that a preoccupation with desires while disregarding other people may be an evidence of self-centeredness, but pretending we aren't driven by internal longings is absurd. Christ called us to himself on the basis of our thirsts: "If anyone thirsts, let him come to me" (John 7:37). Your innermost being is a rich place of passion and longing. If you neglect it, you lose an essential aspect of your humanity. Remember, at times Christ was motivated through his longings. For example, during the Last Supper he said, "I've had a deep desire to eat this Passover with you before I suffer" (Luke 22:15, GW). He was fueled by a desire for intimacy and a chance to speak into the lives of those he deeply loved. He may have awoken in the middle of the night and envisioned the looks on the faces of his disciples when he spoke caringly to them. Longing may have filled his heart as he passionately yearned for the depth of connection he would know with them on that day. If we renew our thoughts, we will never understand the heart that drives our minds and actions. We are fully capable of doing and thinking all the right things and still living from a deadened or corrupt heart.

THE HEART OF DESIRE

———— ·•· ————

"I'm learning to pay attention to my stomach and actually eat when I am hungry. Throughout my life I refused to allow myself to acknowledge that my stomach was growling. I would get mad at being hungry and having to take time to eat. I felt restricted, inconvenienced, and not in control. To acknowledge my appetite is terrifying. To not acknowledge it made me stuff everything way down. By doing that, I was destroying myself. God designed me to crave food."

—A recovering anorexic

DO YOU KNOW WHAT YOU WANT?

———— ·•· ————

You would not be in pain in your marriage if you didn't want something from your spouse. What you want may not be clear to you and may not be easy to articulate. Yet when you take a careful look, you will discover that your pain is fueled by intense desire. What you will find is that your heart has a hope for a relational depth and connection that cannot be dismissed. In order to understand the emotional turmoil and agony you are experiencing in your marriage, you will need to clarify the deep, motivating appetites God has placed within your heart.

You may be thinking, *What appetites? I'm not asking for much. I just want to be happy.* Don't trivialize your heart in that way—you are designed to want much more. What moves you? Music, injustice, sex, worship, nature, the Super Bowl? Think of a time when you have been aware of something inside you coming alive in response to God, beauty, or tragedy. Why are you moved by the frightened eyes of a hungry child standing alone and lost, a richly colored sunset on a crisp autumn evening, or an old song that brings sentimental remembrances of a time when life was good? Your heart is potent with powerful appetites that are released when they are accessed by meaningful encounters. Stirrings from deep within your heart move you, and while they may not be easy to articulate, they motivate almost everything you do. God knows we have these nonverbal thirsts that can best be understood as "groanings."

> Likewise the Spirit helps us in our weakness. For we do not know what to pray for as we ought, but the Spirit himself intercedes for us with groanings too deep for words. (Romans 8:26)

CHAMBERS OF THE HEART

Chambers, caverns, where springs of water burst forth, where our secrets are, where our groans come from, where painful memories reside, where we long to be whole. This is a powerful place that is hidden even from us. We fear our rage; we fear our passions.

We think we can explain and articulate passion and desire. When we ask people what they really want, we are forcing them to fabricate or use words to express what only the heart knows. This is why we are confused as we try to clarify the sounds and groans of our innermost being. "I want significance, meaning, love, integrity." Do these words do justice to the vibrant chambers of our hearts? Not even close.

Whoa! Where are you going with this, Mike? Is this some sort of postmodern stuff about words not really having meaning? No, that's not it at all. *Are you saying we have inarticulate hearts with yearnings that will forever remain mysterious, even to us?* Yes, that is exactly what I am saying. The millions of descriptive words that have been written to try to represent the inner workings of our hearts have all been mere approximations of the ineffable. *So why should you try to add more confusion?* Because we must come to grips with the powerful forces within us that drive us in directions that often don't make sense. Paul said, "For I do not do the good I want, but the evil I do not want is what I keep on doing" (Romans 7:19).

This verse has been interpreted in many different ways, but Paul was clearly acknowledging that the drives and forces within him warred against his clearly articulated intentions. Our goal is to acknowledge and understand what drives us, even if we cannot always clearly verbalize what comes from our hearts. We should never try to categorize or systematize our thirsts and longings with the belief that they can become perfectly clear and tangible. As you read this chapter, be aware that what is driving you is far more powerful than your understanding will allow. The compelling groanings come from what we describe as the "chambers of the heart." "The purpose in a man's heart is like deep water, but a man of understanding will draw it out" (Proverbs 20:5).

Chuck and I recently had our annual boys' day out. As things have worked out, his grandson, Noah, and my son, Carmen, are the same age. Each year the four of us spend a day together doing guy stuff. Last summer we decided to visit the World War II submarine the USS Cod. I've seen many movies with submarines in them and was prepared for a time of claustrophobia as I pictured squeezing into the cramped, oppressive quarters inside the submarine. Still, I was looking forward to our time together.

We arrived at the harbor, and after shooting all the enemy planes from the surface guns of the sub, we went down the stairs into the heart of the ship. Rather than feeling cramped and claustrophobic, I was surprised to find that not only did I have plenty of headroom but I felt at ease in the expanse of the large submarine. As we explored the interior, the sections of the vessel seemed to go on and on. The intricacies of the machinery, weaponry, living quarters, and command sections were fascinating, each new area adding to the depth and complexity of the amazing underwater ship. We ended up spending much more time in the sub than we would have thought and realized we had just begun to appreciate the capabilities it held.

The chambers of your heart are much like a submarine. You have been designed with capacities and desires that appear to be easily understood when looked at from the surface, but as you enter into them, you find a depth and complexity you hadn't anticipated. It is from these amazing chambers that the thirsts of the soul emerge. When Paul talked about "groaning" in 2 Corinthians 5, he was alluding to desires that come from distress within these intricate and powerful chambers. Taking the time to explore the chambers of desire within your heart will help you understand the battle raging in your soul and lead to hope and thriving.

Picture your body as a hill in a mountain range. In the middle of the hill is a small opening, the entrance into a vast cavern, or what we call a chamber. The opening of the cavern is somewhat small and dimly lit. But beyond the opening, the chamber expands and seems endless. From the vast region beyond the opening you hear faint sounds, inarticulate groanings, and melodious flowing water, and you sense a mysterious wealth of something you can't quite make out. You have entered into the chambers of your heart. Within these chambers are your desires for love, purpose, and integrity. You are continually managing your life in response to these desires.

THE CHAMBERS OF THE UNCORRUPTED, PURE, OR "GOOD" HEART

Difficult marriages take a toll on a person's identity. Questions arise such as, *Am I lovable? Am I just trying to express myself, or am I as disagreeable as he says I am? Am I trying to offer leadership, or am I as selfish and controlling as she tells me I am? What am I supposed to want from my spouse and my marriage? I feel like I've lost myself, so who am I?* The heart becomes confused.

As we counsel people who have been involved in tough marriages, we find they have lost perspective on who they are and what a healthy marriage feels and looks like. This is why we need to spend time clarifying so that confusion can be minimized. The key to clarifying is to develop a healthy picture and understanding of a godly marriage. We can study Scripture and listen to wise mentors to get a head knowledge of what a good marriage looks like, but without experiencing an understanding, knowledge will be minimally helpful. The place to experience an understanding is in the heart.

As you speak from the richness of the chambers of your heart, you want to feel the purity of your passion. Yet as we are discovering, the journey into our desires is painful. As you discover what your heart desires, you become more keenly aware of what your spouse is not fulfilling and where you have failed to fulfill your mate.

A brief study of Genesis 2 will give us an idea of God's design for the chambers of our souls. To understand the concept of desire or thirst, we must realize that if we are full we are not thirsty or hungry. On Thanksgiving, when I (Mike) finish my second helping of Nonny Great's Italian recipe stuffing, delicately roasted fresh turkey, and Lin's incomparable gravy, I don't hunger and thirst for more. I am satiated and have no craving for a third helping. I hunger and thirst, however, on Thanksgiving morning when I am awakened with the smell of roasting turkey. I experience the desire when my olfactory senses are enticed, resulting in the chambers of my empty stomach groaning for satisfaction.

God created Adam knowing fullness (as opposed to emptiness) of heart. The life he provided was so satisfying that Adam did not know what it meant to hunger and thirst for what he did not have. The chambers of Adam's heart were in a perpetual state of fulfillment, so he was able to continually express his manhood from the power and strength of full chambers. For example, since God gave Adam the task of caring for the Garden, it implies that he had a capacity, or a chamber in his heart, for meaning, *purpose*, or significance. When Adam worked in the garden, he felt total satisfaction in his heart's chamber designed for purpose because he was able to fulfill God's blueprint within him.

God told Adam to live with integrity within a moral framework. He was designed to experience *integrity* within himself by obeying God's moral plan and by not eating the fruit that was forbidden. By obeying God, Adam could delight in his capacity, or heart chamber, that expressed and experienced moral purity and integrity. He would also delight in the just design of the world in which God placed him. Evil had not tarnished the purity and goodness of the environment Adam and Eve knew.

An implication can be drawn from Genesis that God designed a third capacity within men and women—the capacity for *relationship* with God and people. Adam experienced such deep satisfaction in his heart's relational chamber with his intimate communion with God that he was completely unaware of another dimension in the design of that chamber: relationship with a woman. God tasked Adam with naming the animals he had created partly to develop awareness that he was alone and desired a woman with flesh to satisfy relational intimacy. When God created Eve, Adam's heart was ecstatic and deeply fulfilled by the one-flesh intimacy he experienced with his wife.

Before Adam and Eve sinned, they experienced deep satisfaction within the chambers of their hearts. They knew what it was like to love and to be loved with utter purity. Expressions of love and joint purpose within a moral framework were offered to each other and to God without shame or fear. The heart was a place where the joy of life was continually known. It is important to know that God's design for your heart is good. Like Adam and Eve, you are fearfully and wonderfully made with incredible richness and depth.

When Adam and Eve decided to run their own lives and violate relationship with God, something tragic happened within the chambers of their hearts. Rather than being a place where joy and satisfaction were known, fear, shame, and emptiness were found. Adam and Eve covered themselves because they feared and mistrusted each other. They avoided and dreaded God because he could expose the corruption that had replaced the purity within their hearts. The first couple had betrayed all the goodness God had designed them with and entrusted to them, resulting in devastatingly corrupted hearts. What was once a place of fullness and contentment became a place of emptiness, turmoil, and desire. After the fall of mankind, men and women would hunger and cry out for loving relationships, meaning and purpose, and justice and moral integrity.

THE HEART'S CHAMBERS:
DESIRES FOR RELATIONSHIP, PURPOSE, AND INTEGRITY

God designed us with capacities, or chambers in our hearts, for *relationship*, *purpose*, and *integrity*, which we experience and express through longing and desire.

The Relationship Chamber

We long to find completion in relationship by joining with a life mate. A man and a woman desire a soul connection where they can offer themselves and receive one another. They want to be utterly known in the most profound ways. They want to be able to fail and still be loved, to be ugly and yet pursued.

Women especially want to be pursued and "entered" so they may experience and express the beauty of God's image within them. A woman often asks, "Do I have the beauty that compels you to pursue me?" As Larry Crabb said in his interview series *A Liberating Look at Gender*, "A woman says, 'I want to invite you to experience the beauty in the depths of my being.'"[2] A healthy woman has a confidence that she has something attractive and powerful within her that will be fully released when a strong husband engages her heart. She desires that her man offer his strength so she can respond and envelop him with the magnificence of her being. She does not fear his masculinity nor think of herself as inferior or superior to him. Rather than desire to be taken care of, she longs for the love, security, and resources of a husband in order to provide the safety and stability that free her to abandon her fears and make available the splendor of God's beauty within her.

The Purpose Chamber

We also desire that our lives and our marriages have meaning and purpose. The world may struggle with believing in ultimate purpose and meaning, but our hearts desire that our marriages provide lasting significance. We long to be valued and pursued as men and women by a spouse who shares our desires and unites with us in purpose. God's design is that our marriages signify the relationship Christ, the bridegroom, has with his bride, the church. This culminates in the idea of looking back from old age and delighting in the lasting legacy our marriage has made in the lives of our family and others.

As Crabb suggests, men especially want to know they have something powerful within them that they can pour into their wives' hearts so they can express the strength of God's image within them. As Crabb states, "A man, can he believe, does he know that there's something alive within him, that when he moves toward his wife, toward his friend, toward his son or daughter, that something incredibly powerful pours out of the depths of his being, and it reaches the heart of the other, and it stimulates, (it doesn't create), life in the other?"[3]

A man is always asking the question, "Do I have what it takes to make a positive difference in your life?" A healthy man has a confidence that he has a potency of life that has a profound effect on his wife. Rather than seeking assurance and validation for insecure manhood, he desires to offer his strength to a wife who will delight in being moved by his masculinity. He is not interested in dominating or controlling but seeks to offer God's strength to influence and make a life-enhancing difference in his wife that elicits her respect for him.

The Integrity Chamber

Deep connection is founded on unshakeable trust. We long for a spouse who will never betray us, never use our weakness against us, and never grow weary of the beauty and strength within us. Our hope is that our spouse will offer us an integrity we have found in no other person. We desire to journey through life with a spouse who knows us in the deepest sense, accepts our flaws, and delights in our strengths. We long to find that same integrity within ourselves.

Men and women who offer each other integrity are healthy enough to be honest about the good, bad, ugly, and beautiful within them and their spouses. Since their identity is firmly established in the work and love of Christ within their hearts, they are free to embrace their humanness and not pretend they are any better or worse than they are. People with hearts of integrity do not have hidden agendas or manipulative ways. They make sure their spouses never have reason to question the sincerity of their hearts nor their commitment to the covenant made before God. And when there is failure, the offended husband or wife will strongly rebuke, forgive, and do the sacrificial work of restoration. The offending spouse will take full responsibility, experience remorse, repent, receive forgiveness, and do the hard work of restoration. Where there are past or present wounds, a heart of integrity is willing to enter the wounds of their hurting mate with offers of hope and healing. A marriage filled with integrity involves a husband and wife who believe they are *for* (not against) one another and *for* God's good purposes for their union. Above all, they desire God's goodness and glory to be expressed and experienced in their marriage.

You may be thinking that all of this is too idealistic and not anywhere near where your heart is. But did you feel a resonating agreement in your heart when you read about the uncorrupted desires that exist in a healthy heart? If you did, your heart stirred because the chambers of your heart are designed to crave these things. As we shall discover later, the world and the Enemy have assaulted your heart so these desires often are hidden in the darkest recesses of your chambers. In the midst of your pain and confusion, please believe these healthy thirsts exist behind your fear, bitterness, and despair. With Christ's help, they can be reclaimed and joyfully embraced. Our identities and wholeness can begin to be reclaimed when we are able to embrace the deepest desires of our hearts. Our hope is that you will feel you have permission to explore the deepest regions of your heart so you will have a place to begin "thriving despite."

"One Flesh" — Desiring Completion, Enjoyment, and Enhancement

Scripture teaches that marriage means a husband and wife, though distinct and unique, will become "one flesh."

> For this cause shall a man leave his father and mother, and shall be joined unto his wife, and they two shall be one flesh. This is a great mystery: but I speak concerning Christ and the church. (Ephesians 5:31-32, kjv)

In order to further clarify what is going on in your heart, let's look at how God designed a thirst for relationship, integrity, and purpose. These are expressed in marriage as desires to journey through life experiencing the "one flesh" pursuits of "Completion, Enjoyment, and Enhancement."

In their book *Intimate Allies*, Dan Allender and Tremper Longman express this:

> The purpose of every marriage is to shape the raw material of life to reveal more fully the glory of God. Either we labor to enhance glory, or we exploit the beauty of creation for our pride and pleasure. Every marriage moves toward either creativity or exploitation.[4]

As you are limited within yourself, you want to join with another to offer and receive the uniqueness each has so you can accomplish that which cannot be done alone (conceiving children, growing through the phases of life, etc.). You also long to enjoy the wonder and the mystery of God's gift to you. Your good heart wants to experience and express the beauty and strength that reflects the dignity and glory of God. You long to be with a mate who also has these desires for you.

No one has to be married. A meaningful existence can be enjoyed without a husband or wife. An entire generation is questioning the value of marriage as it sees difficult marriages ending in divorce or surviving in disharmony. Paul even said that for the sake of following Christ it is better to not marry. An individual does not *need* to have a wife or husband to be intact, just like God did not *need* to create people in order to experience being whole or fulfilled. But out of the depth of the mystery of the Trinity came a desire to become one with created beings who shared God's nature but were also very different and distinct from him. In the same way, within each person is a compelling desire to unite with someone who is like them but also completely different. Why? Because relationships and deep connection with others are an integral part of who God is and how he has designed his creations.

Picture someone giving you a large, lightweight, portable mirror that you can easily place in a chair across from you at meals. It's on the other side of your bed when you sleep, and you carry it with you when you go for walks. In it you can clearly see a person who is continually looking at you and in complete harmony with every move you make. The person never causes conflict, requires nothing of you, and leaves your existence undisturbed. Your companion is reliable and safe but is utterly incapable of adding anything to your life. If you sing a song, cook a meal, or utter romantic words, the reflected image has no ability to validate or see worth in anything you may offer.

The image cannot hear or feel you, nor can it speak to you or touch your body so you can be stimulated and respond. Your soul longs for a being who is not vacant and powerless to add to your offering but rather can respond to you with thoughts, emotions, and physicality that you are incapable of generating yourself. The design God has placed within you longs to unite with a soul who is separate and distinct yet works in harmony with you. The result of the interaction with another is an experience of life that is not possible without the other. Even God chose to create humans where he would offer dimensions of his being that were not expressed within the holiness of the Trinity.

I don't think anyone can fully understand why God would disrupt the awesome harmony and peace that existed within the Trinity in order to have relationships with human beings. Think about it: God, who also is fueled by desire, wanted something so deeply that he was willing to create a being who would cause such deep conflict that God would have to undergo torture, mutilation, and death in order to sustain relationships with his creations. He would even alienate himself from himself on the cross, being willing to disrupt the harmony within the Trinity. What would cause him to go to such extreme lengths?

The answer is the desire to be "one" with his creation, offering and receiving what would not occur without being in relationship with someone who is "other" than him. Are you starting to understand? God was whole within himself but desired "another" in order to express that wholeness. *Grace and gratitude work together to unite God and man for eternal relationship, justice, and purpose.* If God went to such extremes to be able to experience this sort of unique "oneness," we must believe the drive for this experience is hidden powerfully within our hearts as well.

Completion

"He that loveth his wife loveth himself" (Ephesians 5:28, KJV).

Marriage is a journey. We travel with our spouses through many phases and changes life brings our way. Two naive, idealistic, wounded people unite and are strengthened, beaten, and changed by the many challenges brought by family, career, health, God's leadings, and the Enemy's attacks. The ups and downs of life provide a setting where a husband and wife weave their lives together. On the day we unite our lives before God, we are "one flesh" in his sight, and on our wedding night we experience that oneness physically. We complete each other at that time. But the wedding day does not yield a final result as much as it sets into motion a lifelong process where love calls us to weave a powerful existence of oneness. Two unique and different souls unite in purpose so that they join together to function as a complete entity.

When I (Mike) was in undergraduate school, I met with one of my professors who had become a mentor to me. As we talked about life, philosophy, and art, he asked me if I had ever heard of German Lieder. I told him I hadn't, which served as an invitation for him to play a record (yes, a *record*) of Dietrich Fischer-Dieskau, a baritone who was considered the world's foremost Lieder singer, accompanied by Gerald Moore. After listening to fifteen seconds of the first song, I was captivated and uttered, "What is this? I have to have it!" I had been introduced to the exquisite expression of a musician communicating the unity and completeness of a fine poet and extraordinary composer. As I began to study Lieder, I grew to understand why it had gripped me so.

Lieder is a collaboration of two completely different forms of artistic expression: music and poetry. Each form has richness and worth and is capable of standing alone. Yet when they are combined, a profundity of expression is reached that transcends each contributor. A composer, such as Franz Schubert, is drawn to a poem by a writer, such as Heinrich Heine or Goethe, and "enters into" the creative thought expressed in his words. As he is moved and inspired by the essence of the poem, he begins to bring musical expression to it, adding dimensions and colors words cannot express. The poem is not intruded upon or misused in any way. Rather its essence is appreciated and united with the inspiration of the composer to form a more complete expression of the creative idea. It is the task of the singer to allow himself to be an instrument for the communication of the oneness or completion of the creative inspiration.

We had the privilege of watching our mother and father spend years weaving their lives together and completing each other. Our parents had many similarities but also some strong differences. Mom was raised in a family with a strict Protestant heritage, while Dad's family was Catholic in tradition but alcoholic and abusive in practice. What they both brought into marriage were significant health problems and a short life expectancy. We were raised with an understanding that our parents had illnesses that would take their lives prematurely and without warning. Despite having a heart that was severely damaged from youth, limiting her endurance and activity, Mom had to work in order to help support a family with six children. We saw how Dad completely understood her limitations, filled in where she faltered, and encouraged her when she struggled. Mom understood that a man operating with only two-thirds of a lung and severe heart damage needed to pace himself and would always live in frustration, aware of the physical strength he did not have. She helped when he was depleted and gave him hope when he was discouraged. Often without words they functioned as one as they dealt with the problems of having a large family, limited income, and damaged bodies.

The concept of a husband and a wife completing each other in such a way as to create something new that would not be possible without the complementary resources of both is exemplified by the new life that results from sexual union. The life force within a woman receives the potent, life-giving energies of her husband and joins with them so that new life, transcending the limitations of both of them, is created. The physical creation of a child can also serve as a metaphor for the spiritual, emotional, and practical creative results of a husband and wife who complete each other. Our hearts are designed to yearn for that type of completion.

Enjoyment

Every once in a while God speaks directly to me. He usually uses a two-by-four to rap against my head in order to get my attention so I will listen — but he speaks. When Lin and I had been married for about ten years, I had an encounter with God. Having studied, read about, and taught on marriage, I believed I knew how to have a healthy marriage. The problem was that Lin wasn't following the game plan and fulfilling the role I had imagined for her. In my frustration I cried out to God that I didn't know how to love her when she wouldn't respond to my noble efforts. *Whack!* After He cleared my head of my own foolishness he said, "Love her? You don't even know who she is. You have been so busy trying to make her into who you want her to be that you have not bothered to explore the mystery of the gift I have given you. She holds a beauty and depth that you will never see until you drop your agenda for her and allow yourself to be captivated by her."

I began to see how my efforts to "love" my wife were filled with manipulations to turn her into the woman who fit my ideal and my concept of what she should be like. By doing so, I was unable to appreciate who she was. Lin is an East Coast Italian-Catholic who comes from an extraverted, liberal, quick-witted, success-driven, intellectual family. I am a Midwestern Slovenian Protestant who comes from an introverted, blue-collar, cautious, conservative family, whose parents never finished high school. I wanted to shape her into a person with the characteristics of my family instead of appreciating and exploring her differences. God began releasing a longing to move beyond my insecurities and discover the mysteries within my wife. As you can imagine, God has had to use the same two-by-four on several occasions.

In marriage we join with a distinct "other." Rather than selfishly and foolishly trying to compel your spouse to be like you or who you want him or her to be, the joy of a healthy marriage is to spend a lifetime exploring and enjoying the mystery of a unique soul who is God's gift to you. Instead of being alienated by differences, learning to appreciate how your spouse thinks, laughs, cries, experiences sexuality, and grapples with life can lead to a profound "one-flesh" relationship. And, yes, rather than conforming to all the expectations your spouse may have of you, invite him or her into your world. God wants you to connect in the deepest chambers of your heart—mentally, spiritually, and physically.

Spiritually, both husband and wife are created in God's image and display dimensions of who God is. One of the goals of a godly marriage is to live out the wonder of God's personality expressed in the way of enjoyment and appreciation of one another. In a difficult marriage, spouses tend to lose sight of the beauty of God's image existing in each other. Remember that you were built to connect with the other-gendered image of God found in your spouse.

ENHANCING

Enjoying and enhancing work together. The reason we are treating them as separate issues is that most people have an agenda to "enhance" their spouse but are unwilling to accept, appreciate, and enjoy their "otherness." The attempts to help their spouse come more from a corrupt "bad" heart than they do from a pure "good" heart.

Everyone enters marriage shaped by the harshness of a fallen world. As a result, people wear masks, live by fear, have an inflated view of themselves, and basically are works in progress. The apostle Paul told husbands,

> Husbands, love your wives, as Christ loved the church and gave himself up for her, that he might sanctify her, having cleansed her by the washing of water with the word, so that he might present the church to himself in splendor, without spot or wrinkle or any such thing, that she might be holy and without blemish. (Ephesians 5:25-27)

If you're able to recognize dignity in your spouse, your desire will be to enhance that dignity so it more clearly reflects the nature of God. You'll desire to develop and enhance your mate's ability and capacity for relational depth, purpose and meaning in life, and holy living. As you see her wounds and insecurities, a vision of who she could become when her full beauty and strength are realized guides your interactions. A longing for his wholeness emerges from the depths of the chambers of your heart and deepens your appreciation for what God is doing in your spouse's life. This longing is the driving force behind "others-centered love." In a healthy marriage, both spouses allow themselves to be stretched and enhanced as their beloved enters the chambers of their heart. (A note of caution: A godly desire to enhance your spouse cannot come from a self-centered, corrupted heart. Husbands who enhance come from a stance of a humble student, always learning who their spouses are and what has made them who they are. Their own heart's agenda has been clarified and cleansed so they love from a pure heart. In most difficult marriages, a person cannot love in this way because pain and confusion often get in the way.)

As you continue to journey through this book, our hope is that by the time you get to the chapter on the "Thriving Heart" you'll feel confident that your desires are being clarified, you'll be disengaging from the corruption in your marriage, and you'll find it is possible to love from a good heart.

CHAPTER 4

Difficult Spouses

If possible, so far as it depends on you, live peaceably with all.
— Romans 12:18

The battle you fight isn't casual. You may be married to someone who is really tough to live with and poses serious problems. Difficult marriages result when difficult people come together under one roof. Living with a difficult spouse may be more challenging than you ever imagined. Part of the pain of living with a difficult spouse is that other people in your life may have little awareness that he or she is difficult. You have a public face you offer to others and a private face you turn toward your spouse. You encounter a face your spouse shows to no one else. Few people can understand the battle within another's marriage. Difficult spouses may appear to be loving and caring to others but can be cold or cruel to their mate. This makes the journey even more lonely.

A difficult spouse poses severe obstacles to intimacy. As we will discuss later, freedom comes from accepting (not necessarily approving of) who your spouse is and giving up an agenda to make him or her change.

Q: "I thought you said the problem we face is how we cope with not getting what we want. If that is the case, why are you going to talk about the issues we have with our spouse?"

It's always interesting how people in counseling talk about problems with their spouses who are not in counseling. Some just blast away and paint a picture of their spouses as the most despicable, unloving human beings imaginable. Others, well schooled in the "don't-blame-your-problems-on-someone-else" teachings think they are copping out or even betraying their spouses if they portray them in a critical light. They wonder, *How can I describe my husband without disrespecting him?* Still others test the waters to see how much they are "allowed" to say about the one who they believe is causing them pain. The truth is that all experienced marriage counselors know there are two sides to every story, and the whole story cannot come out by talking to only one spouse. But what is essential is that you're free to describe the reality you live with from your perspective. In order to thrive you must be able to face the good, bad, ugly, and beautiful about yourself, your spouse, and your marriage.

A blueprint for a difficult spouse doesn't exist. Remember we have said that difficult spouses range from *good but flawed* to *evil and destructive*. We are going to discuss three categories for difficult spouses. Many more could be described, but these three will give you a start on understanding some of the reasons you've been unable to resolve differences with your spouse. Some difficult spouses may be limited in their abilities and capacities for relationship. Others may have given up the hard work of marriage and have rejected their spouse. The most destructive kind, though, is the dangerous spouse who seeks to harm or destroy his or her mate. These spouses are emotionally, spiritually, or physically abusive and will be discussed in chapter 6 about dangerous spouses.

By now you may be starting to see the problems in your marriage in a different light. We want you to see them in a new way so you have another approach to understanding what you are struggling with and who you are married to. You may say,

Q. *"I get that. I know I'm not getting what I want nor giving what I want. Instead I'm getting what I don't want and having*

*to give what I don't want. So what do I do about it? How do I fix
this and start thriving? If I don't get a divorce and trying harder
isn't the answer, then what's the next step?"*

The next step is committing to going slowly and thoughtfully.
After identifying some of the problems, we're going to keep deepening
your understanding of what you want and who you are married to.

Let's talk about the first category of difficult spouses, which will
describe a person who may be trying to have a good marriage but who
lacks the capacity or ability to address marital issues and needs. This is
best described as the spouse with limited capacities.

LIMITED CAPACITIES

Everyone has strengths and limitations. Initially, we may have been
drawn to our spouse because of his or her God-given gifts and strengths.
"She is wonderful because she is so caring." "He is so funny and is great
to be around." "What insight and understanding she has!" "He is the
most responsible person I know." We tend to enjoy a person's positive
qualities and then attempt to build a relationship around them. But we
forget to really look at a person's limitations and how that will affect
the quality of the relationship. A person's limitations pose problems in
relationships and impede growth.

It is important for you to know your spouse well enough to understand what he or she is able to offer you and what he or she doesn't have
the ability to give. When you ask something from your spouse in the
area of his limitations, what you want from him is not available. You
don't get it from your spouse because he cannot give what he doesn't
have. You may think he has it, but he doesn't. He may have given you
hints or tidbits of it, but it's not there. For example, your dad may have
been a great "fix it" guy, and you thought your well-tooled and well-
intentioned husband should be able to repair anything just like your

dad, but he can't. His heart may be willing and he might spend hours trying, but he is inept. He will not satisfy your desire for resting in the comfort of a man you can admire because he can tackle any household problem. (Yes, we sometimes write from our own lives. Why do you think we're psychologists instead of home builders, like our dad wanted us to be?)

Not only does your spouse have limits in her ability to give, but she also may be limited in what she is able to receive from you. Many people simply are unable to allow themselves to be loved. You can learn to communicate in the most insightful, loving ways and your spouse may not be able to receive the love you offer. And conversely, you may drop all your defenses and articulate your needs clearly, and she still may not be able to respond to what it is you are longing for. While everyone has limitations, some difficult spouses have deficits that are the source of great pain in a marriage. You may have dreamed about a wife who loves romantic walks and lots of attention. Yet for many reasons, your wife is very shy and grows uncomfortable when the focus is on her. This includes your focus. She doesn't choose to be cold or unresponsive; since she was a child she has lacked the capacity to receive and enjoy attention. Though she has worked hard to change, she is only minimally more able to receive than when you were first married, possibly many years ago.

You need to explore the common question regarding a limited spouse: Is it that he *can't* address your needs or *won't* address them? You may assume that he is resisting you and is refusing to expend the effort to meet your need, when, as in our examples just given, he is actually unable to respond in a way that makes you feel loved and heard. If you are trying to clarify your understanding of why your marriage is difficult, it is critical that you consider the possibility that your spouse cannot respond to you as you desire.

When a person has an obvious physical, intellectual, or emotional restriction, such limitations are not difficult to accept when they are apparent. A tone-deaf husband will not be able to engage your desire to join him in careful, nuanced expressions while singing vocal duets.

A color-blind wife will be limited in her ability to appreciate your excitement over the brilliance of the leaves changing from green to bright red to a glowing yellow before they say farewell with brown during fall. The types of limitations we're going to describe, however, are harder to accept and understand. As hard as it may be to accept, some of the difficulties caused by a limited spouse are not personal in nature. They aren't a response to you. They occur because of who your spouse is. Suffering due to a spouse with limitations is real but of a different nature than pain felt from a rejecting or dangerous mate. Many limited spouses have paid the price for their lack of ability by having to hear accusations of being uncaring, irresponsible, or selfish.

Limitations are just what the word implies: limits. When a person has reached his or her limit, nothing more is available. Limitations require that you accept that some things in the marriage will not change short of divine intervention. A short person will not become tall. A superficial person is not likely to become deep. While everyone has limitations in his or her abilities to relate and function with others, some people have limitations that are better described as *impairments*. In marriage, such limitations may impair the ability to give and receive, limiting the possibility for deep, rich growth and bonding. If the desire of your heart is to join in an intimate way, limitations will inflict pain and wounds in the core of your soul. Your heart cries out, *Why can't you see . . . ? Why do you always . . . ? When will you ever . . . ?* The answer to your plea is often silence, and your desires go unmet. Your thirst for closeness becomes a source of pain, resulting in groaning for what you cannot have. The hurt is a result of limitations in your spouse that are experienced as rejection or lack of love. Recognizing and accepting these deficits is crucial to a healthy marriage.

Every marriage is comprised of two limited people who are mismatched to some degree. This is true from design. Men and women seem to see and engage in life from different perspectives and with different capacities. These differences are not trivial, as they limit your ability to strongly connect. In counseling couples, it is clear to us that even those who are well read on marriage have difficulty accepting their spouse's limitations and differences or "otherness." This is because your soul's longings cannot be silenced, and you resist embracing the reality that your spouse has limits.

Humans have many areas where we are limited. Here are three specific limitations that cause confusion as well as pain in a difficult marriage.

Limited Capacity for Understanding

People who are limited in understanding just don't get it. They may go to growth seminars or learn the relational jargon, but they can't understand the words and concepts they articulate. Their ability to see things from another's perspective is minimal. They can be characterized from being "simple and harmless" all the way to being "brilliant and lethal." A woman's needs may be trivialized because her husband simply cannot comprehend that a woman's sensitivities are different from his. I have counseled with men whose crude language has clearly offended and unsettled their wives. More than one man has said with genuine surprise, "I don't know why that would bother her. It never bothers the guys at work. What's the big deal?" Knowing that his wife is troubled by his coarseness, he may be simpleminded and try to lightly tease her with rough language because he doesn't get how much it bothers her, or if he is shrewd, he could use his coarseness to torment her, minimizing her discomfort because her response isn't logical to him.

Others with limited understanding do not learn from experience. Their fixed way of viewing things is not influenced by others' reactions to them. One woman I talked with could not understand why her husband stopped socializing with her, including not attending the same church. She was hurt and angry that he didn't care about how he was hurting her. When he gave his perspective, he said they couldn't go anywhere without her being critical and setting a negative tone, making going out a miserable experience. She found fault with the script of the movie, the pastor's message, the salad dressing, the decor of the home—you name it, she criticized it. They had lost relationships with family and friends because people were tired of her not-so-subtle fault-finding messages. She was bewildered that her husband saw her that way. She viewed herself as a person with discernment who simply saw things others didn't see. She could not understand how difficult she was to be with and lacked the ability to receive someone else's perspective.

A person with limited insight does not see his or her role in inter-personal conflict. Blowing things out of proportion, blame shifting, refusing to take responsibility, and being out of control emotionally is harmful to a marriage. But such behaviors make sense to this impaired individual. Her spouse lives with frustration because common sense and simple problem-solving skills are not exercised.

People with limited understanding often lack social intelligence, self-awareness, and the ability to distinguish the greater good from the desire to be right. They tend to miss the longings of their spouse's heart because they don't share the same desires. They are unable to discern a casual request from a critical expression of need and so can't tune in to what really matters to their spouse. Unfortunately, the "big picture" is not understood. Spouses with limited insight tend to create tension, fighting unproductive battles. This person is often content to win the little battles in marriage and doesn't realize he is losing the war to keep his wife's heart. Even after she leaves he remains confused. They lack the ability to move beyond their needs or perspectives to see the greater good.

Limited Capacity for Emotional Expression

In discussing this limitation, we move from the head to the heart. Whereas people with limited understanding can't connect with or deeply appreciate their spouse's needs or perspectives, those with limited capacities for expression have difficulties appropriately engaging in the emotional, creative, and spiritual sensibilities of their spouse. The range for this limitation runs from the soul who is closed off and unable to receive and express love, to the "dullard" who lacks sensitivity, to the one who is out of control and inappropriately expressive.

Many people are limited in their ability to experience and express emotions. They just don't feel strongly about much of anything. They may lack passion and avoid excitement. Being married to a person like this will always result in feeling lonely and empty. It is hard to feel alive and warm with a spouse who can't share your excitement for life. They tend to ask little of their spouses, so you'll always feel like you have much more to give than your mate can receive.

In the beginning of the section on limited capacities we gave an example of a shy wife who was unable to receive her husband's affection or respond with warm engagement from her own heart. Everyone who gets married has a history. Each person enters marriage with wounds that pose some problem in his or her capacity for emotional expression and engagement. Your limited spouse has a story that shaped him or her and helped develop limited capacities.

Our mother's father walked out on five kids when she was only two. Her mother's health was so bad that she was unable to care for her children. Our mom was taken in and raised by an aunt. While the aunt was a loving person, our mother was never quite accepted as a sister by her eight cousins, a fact we were constantly reminded of at large family gatherings until her death. Our grandmother died when our mother was fourteen, and our grandfather died without ever reconciling with the family.

Mom was wounded and limited in her ability to form trusting, deep relationships. Yet no one would know that by being around her. She was happy, outgoing, and everyone's mother. At her funeral, seemingly countless people came up to tell us what a loving mother she had been to them. Yet our mother had a limitation. There was a reserve about her that only those who longed to connect deeply with her would know. She joked and jousted to maintain distance. Love was expressed by action and not words. Underlying so much of her communication was the message, *I care for you and am willing to serve you in any way I can.* This was followed by another message: *But I will be in control and keep a safe distance from you.* Her wounds limited her ability to have an intimate, mutual relationship. She had to be in charge and keep her heart behind a wall of protection. It was only as we began to understand her wounds that we could accept her limitations. We all have wounds and, therefore, we all have limitations.

Many wounds have to do with sexuality. Sexual wounds may come from parents who communicate to their children that sex is somehow bad or dirty and should be feared rather than enjoyed. Others have been wounded by sexual betrayal and abuse. Sadly, for many people, even the thought of sexual intimacy brings the experience of shame. What God intended for pleasure has become a source of pain and confusion. Even after working through sexual abuse and finding healing, individuals may be limited in their ability to fully express themselves sexually to their spouse. They may never allow themselves or their spouse to enjoy the depth of beauty God has bestowed upon sexual expression and experience.

Conversely, others with sexual and other trauma in their past cannot regulate their emotional expression and relational appreciation. Their relationships are often characterized by drama and chaos. They are impaired in their expressive and appreciative capacity and create severe difficulties in their marriage. Healthy, loving engagement is rejected as being boring while destructive turbulence ensues.

Limited Capacity for Growth, Ability to Adapt (Unteachable)

Some people don't grow. Their lives are filled with insecurities and fear. Cautious, careful people, they tend to cling to their spouses with dependency and need. Many women are little girls inside who are either looking for their daddy or terrified of being hurt by their big brother. The responsibilities of being a mother and wife are overwhelming to them and they are so needy that little can ever be asked of them. Adult, masculine strength is not responded to with adult, feminine vigor, so a husband never experiences the beauty of womanhood being released by his insecure, clingy wife.

Some men either have had their confidence stripped from them through failure or it never developed. These insecure men are terrified of making a mistake and avoid responsibility by finding a mommy figure who will take care of them and ask little of them. The older these men get, the more rigid they become. Their wives can never relax and go "off duty" because the weight of family is on their shoulders. She never experiences being able to rest in the security of her husband's strength, feeling free to grow and flourish.

People limited in their ability to adapt have few reserves to call on when trouble hits. Conflict paralyzes them. They will either retreat or rage so they can restore order. Their insecurities make it difficult to join with their spouses in life's adventures and challenges. Safe and predictable, they pose severe difficulties to their mates, who hunger for a one-flesh relationship that reflects the glory and majesty of God. They are perceived as "unteachable."

Will and Karen

Will had just graduated from college when he and Karen married. Will was broke and in debt with a few college loans, so he was very careful with his money. Though it wasn't easy, Karen accounted for every penny she spent and agreed to use coupons whenever possible. Will's financial discipline helped him pay off his debts and allowed them to purchase a home.

As his career developed, Will's income increased but his money management never changed. Fifteen years into his marriage, he still scrutinized every purchase Karen made and always pointed out ways she could have saved more money by making wiser purchases. Karen would patiently argue that they were in a different phase of life where they weren't in crisis, having a more than adequate financial profile. She urged him to relax, be thankful for God's blessings, and enjoy their lives and family. His poverty mindset stole the joy from vacations and family meals ("Did you get this on sale?") and made him unable to receive Karen's fun-loving, spontaneous way of living. She had to inhibit a rich part of her nature because of Will's rigidity.

Every healthy person and couple changes and evolves throughout their marriage. Different phases of marriage require a person to adapt and develop new ways of relating to a spouse and life. Will's fastidious ways of managing money made sense when he and Karen were starting out but were harmful to the marriage as it evolved into a new phase. His limited capacity for adapting to change meant that he was unable to receive the creative and uninhibited passions of his growing wife. Instead of offering Karen a man who lived life as a joyous adventure, Will gave her an inflexible, cautious man whose primary yearning was for safety and stability. When challenged, he was utterly incapable of exploring any alternatives to his stifling, tyrannical money-management style. Karen had to accept that her husband was not able to get a new perspective on life. The result was that Karen knew Will would never be able to join her in her journey through life, enjoying and exploring her thoughts and emotions. Though he was a faithful, dependable man, she felt alone, unwanted, and unloved.

Alan and Jan

Jan was grateful because Alan cared for her and understood her. He had come into her life as a knight in shining armor, rescuing her from oppressive parents and a life of conflict. Being told he was "the best thing that ever happened to me," Alan enjoyed giving her attention, driving her where she needed to go, and even cleaning up her credit card debt.

After they married and started a family, they decided it was in their best interest for Alan to get specialized certification in computers so he could advance in the field and provide for their future. Jan agreed she would step up and take charge of running the house for a couple of years while he studied and took a series of difficult tests. Though she was intelligent, capable, and even willing, she could never quite get it together. Without Alan's help, she was flustered and overwhelmed. She needed him to make even the smallest of decisions. Ever apologetic, she exhausted his cell phone minutes with frequent calls seeking advice and reassurance.

Alan was happy to provide strength to Jan when she was a confused, wounded young woman. But ten years had passed, and he longed for a stronger woman who could partner with him in creating a life and future for them and their children. Jan's life worked when she had a strong man who was willing to take responsibility for her. Though it was spiritually and psychologically possible, she lacked the capacity to adapt to a new phase of her life where she could trust the love and care of her husband yet be able to enjoy her own strengths and self-sufficiency. As a result, Alan had to inhibit his own growth and sense of adventure because Jan was not able to receive and adapt to his changes. What she asked of him was the knight in shining armor who didn't require her to be a responsible, womanly helpmate. Though he would always love Jan, he felt a bit used and unfulfilled, never being able to enjoy the depths and beauty of a wise, mature wife. He thought she needed him to take care of her, but she did not have the desire for all he could offer her.

THE REJECTING SPOUSE

While the pain felt from a spouse with limited capacities can cause great grief in the soul, understanding and accepting limitations brings a perspective that helps. You can't give what you don't have. But our second category is for difficult spouses who inflict a pain that is personal and harder to accept. The rejecting spouse doesn't want to give what you desire and isn't interested in what you are offering. This person is able to recognize the desires of the spouse's heart but makes a choice to selfishly reject involvement. Most people marry with the belief that they are wanted. Someone desires who you are and makes the effort to cultivate a relationship. Certainly in the time leading up to marriage you have confidence that you are accepted and enjoyed. Late-night conversations, expressions of longing, and plans for a future promise an ongoing life where both partners in a marriage desire and want to be with each other. Though the world might spin out of control, you believe you can remain secure and at home with the love of your life.

This is why rejection in marriage is more painful than rejection in other relationships. It is deeply disturbing to be rejected by the one person your heart is designed to join with in the most intimate of ways. The disturbance is so devastating because marital rejection almost always involves a humiliating betrayal and the shaming experience of abandonment. In marriage you take the risk of revealing yourself to another person. You expose all that you are physically, emotionally, and spiritually. In a healthy union, a couple develops a strong knowledge of who their mate is. You know each other in ways not possible outside of marriage. Knowledge of your inner being has been entrusted to another. This is why marital rejection is so painful. It's like taking your clothes off in front of your spouse only to see a look of disapproval or disgust in his or her eyes. *"I have seen you, I have known you, and now I no longer want you. I reject you! Go away. You no longer interest me. I have fallen out of love with you."* These terrible messages can run the range from disinterest to disgust. It may be helpful to look at four patterns of rejection.

I Don't Care About You — I Am Indifferent to You!

Messages of disinterest and lack of care may come from gentle hearts that don't intend to do damage. They may not admit or perhaps even consciously know that they are rejecting their spouse. At some point they stopped doing the hard work of growing their marriage. Something became dead inside them toward their spouse. While they may stay committed to the functional part of their relationship, their heart is not available to engage in the life blood of marriage. The good stuff that keeps a relationship vital is withheld, robbing a mate of the possibility of deep fulfillment. They are characterized by *apathy*: Marriage holds no interest or excitement for them. But indifference should not be looked at as being harmless. Many believe the opposite of love isn't hate but rather is apathy.

Not much interested Sean. He didn't ask much of life — just a clean house, decent food, a 52-inch TV, and no hassle. Sex every once in a while was okay—just don't make it complicated. If asked whether or not he loved his wife, he'd sort of grunt something indicating his apathy toward the question. Nothing Terry could say or do would reach him. Counseling, marriage books, or marriage classes at church were not of interest to him. She had put on a bit of weight, and age had altered her looks. She experienced his lack of desire for her as a deep rejection of all she was as a woman. Her future appeared to be one of loneliness without hope of intimate connection with Sean.

I Am Disinterested in You—I'm Too Busy for You!

Since it takes selfless effort to keep marriage fresh and alive, it is even more tiring when a rejecting spouse abandons the mate and becomes unavailable for relationship. A disinterested spouse has often given his heart to something outside the marriage but isn't willing to recognize the impact of his behavior on his spouse. He usually finds justification for staying away: school, church, family, the bar, work—whatever. It is clear, however, that his deepest loyalties are with something or someone else. The unwillingness to remain deeply engaged in marital intimacy for the sake of other interests is experienced as a covert betrayal of wedding vows.

Ginny and Randy

Ginny said she wanted a great marriage—a godly one. Every new book on marriage was on her desk. Others recognized her insight and knowledge and asked her to teach on marriage and godly femininity. She spent hours in preparation for her lessons, which she taught to several groups a week. Taking on the position of Director of Women's Ministries at her large church gave her many opportunities to teach and counsel women. Randy felt he got the leftovers. The passion of her heart was for teaching, not for him. She was better at words than he was, so every attempt to express his concern was met with her brilliant justification for her involvement with ministry. In his heart he knew that her first love was teaching about marriage and not marriage itself. No one could understand how someone with such a great wife could be so unhappy in his marriage. They didn't know that his role in the marriage was to admire his wife without ever being intimately connected with her.

I Don't Like You — I Am Against You!

After many battles and failures in a marriage, resentment and bitterness characterize the heart of many spouses. The feelings of being let down, unappreciated, or used rigidify the heart, and a spouse lives behind a wall of resentment and hostility. The bullets fly and no wound is painful enough. Mates who don't like their husband or wife often attack their spouse's masculine or feminine identity. A woman may reject any trace of her husband's masculinity. She will insist on decorating the house in a completely feminine style. The only place he can call his own and feel masculine is a little corner of the basement where he has a small work area. His interest in sports is chided as something she hopes he will grow out of. Instead of offering her his masculine love, he is reduced to reading her expectations and trying to anticipate what will offend her. He resigns himself to living with a wall of hostility and fighting fantasies of women who invite his love.

Conversely, many wives have husbands who reject and disparage the complexity of their feminine soul. Their hostility is expressed by mocking their wife's emotions and needs. A wife's tears of pain bring rage from her husband's heart. Rather than enjoying the richness of her inner life and the relational dimensions of her feminine soul, he resents being challenged and seeks subservience from his wife. These rejecting husbands tend to diminish their wives by never pursuing their hearts or their minds. As a result, wives don't feel valued by their husbands. Depression or feelings of intense loneliness are common among wives whose husbands dismiss or reject their female strengths.

Ted and Leigh

Ted was in the family room watching a play-off game with a neighbor, his fifteen-year-old son, and one of his son's friends. Popcorn, chips, and glasses of soda generously decorated the floor and tables. As the game was nearing crunch time, his wife, Leigh, came into the room. Her house was prepared for a visit from *House Beautiful* magazine at any moment. In her home there were no laundry piles, no dirty dishes in the sink, and no clutter anywhere. Mercy was not afforded to those who didn't share her need for order and cleanliness. Leigh was upset that the room was untidy and told Ted he had better not leave things in such sad shape.

Ted assured her the guys would straighten up after the game, but Leigh wouldn't leave it alone. The guys were informed that she was tired of having to clean up everyone's mess and being disrespected. Her husband got out of his chair and asked her to come with him into another room. When he requested she let them watch their game and reassured her they would deal with the clutter later, she became deeply hurt. He never listened to her. He never paid attention to what mattered to her. When Ted tried to reassure her again that he would clean everything up, she said she couldn't believe they had made such a mess. Her tone had escalated and everyone could hear her increased agitation. Ted asked her to please stop because she was beginning to cause a scene. Leigh broke into tears and told him he was at fault for causing a scene because he couldn't honor her simple request to clean up the room. Nothing was ever enough for Leigh. She was unpleasable.

Leigh had Ted in a bind. It was like fighting a grappler. A grappler uses any move his opponent makes to pull him in and lock him into a position where escape is impossible. The opponent's offensive efforts are used against him. Leigh was impenetrable and unreachable. Anything Ted said was put in the worst possible light. Any attempt to ask Leigh to consider how she was affecting the others was perceived as an attack. The more he tried, the more Ted experienced frustration and defeat. Leigh was completely focused on her need to have the room cleaned up. Her dislike of Ted was expressed strongly though indirectly. She robbed him of the pretense of masculinity. In his attempts to survive her, Ted turned off the TV, and despite the guys' protests, he cleaned up the room.

I Am Against You — I Loathe You!

Some rejecting spouses justify their actions by finding a flaw and turning against their partners. The rejecting spouse leads his partner to believe that she is defective as a person and should be confronted with her "faults" whenever the chance arises, so she is always being corrected or criticized. The rejecting spouse is often a person who is *done* with the marriage and holds his or her wife or husband responsible. We call this the "get even" survival strategy in chapter 8 on The Surviving Heart. This person has a disdain for the husband or wife. *You will never hurt me again. I'm through with being put down, having trust broken, being taken for granted, having you rage against me anytime I bring up an issue!* — the reasons go on and on. Usually these spouses feel very justified in rejecting their husband or wife and believe he or she is the cause for their unhappiness. Reasonable dialogue to explore issues never occurs. The war for their hearts has been won. Bitterness, anger, and the spirit of unforgiveness have taken up residence and color every interaction with their spouse. Nothing the spouse can do will make a difference. This spouse has hardened his or her heart to the point that there is no way back.

Jim and Abby

Jim announced that the family would not be able to take a vacation this summer. He was sorry, but finances and time just wouldn't allow it. Deeply disappointed, Abby asked if there was any way they could get a little time away. The trap had been set and she had taken the bait. Jim had a response waiting, one that reflected his disdain for her and the pain she had caused him. He relished launching his hatred at her.

"Look, Abby, you're the one who wanted a fourth child. I told you if we did it, there would be no money. You should have thought about this when you were pushing for another kid. I am not going to go into more debt, and I'm not going to work any more overtime. I've given up enough for you and what you want. You and the kids can find stuff to do this summer. You got what you want, now stop pressuring me. If you had listened to me, we'd have the house paid for, I'd be in a job I really like, and we could do whatever we want. Don't blame me because you can't have your vacation."

This person feels no responsibility toward his or her spouse and has basically left the marriage. If he or she is having an affair, the pain of betrayal and rejection is profound. How do you compete with a fantasy lover or a pornographic image? How do you deal with it when your spouse says he or she is staying only for the kids—and means it? You have to watch and ache as your mate's best energies, the ones you long for, are freely offered elsewhere, and he or she does't care how much it hurts you.

This chapter introduced some ways of understanding difficult spouses. In chapter 6 we will take it up a notch and talk about dangerous spouses who cause intense suffering. Before we do, we need to introduce the other side of desire: corruption. Remember that you need to understand whether or not your desires are good. To develop the confidence that your or your spouse's desires are coming from a good heart, you must have the integrity to address your own darkness and distortions.

CHAPTER 5

Corrupted Desires

Keep your heart with all vigilance,
for from it flow the springs of life.
— *Proverbs 4:23*

Jared was clearly hostile to his wife, Stephanie. In their first session of marriage counseling, he expressed that he felt disrespected as a husband because she refused to have sex with him outside of their scheduled Friday night times. Stephanie pointed out that she was not interested in sex but in a counseling session with their pastor had agreed she should not withhold herself and would be intimate with him one night a week. She told him she was not interested in competing with the pornographic images in his mind nor with the three other women he had had affairs with. And, no, she was not involved with any other man. The thought repulsed her. Jared accused her of having an unforgiving heart and being a poor example of a Christian wife.

Stephanie, the eldest of six children, was born to a family where her dad was consumed with his success and left her mom to face the stress of raising six children. A year after Stephanie was born her mother gave birth to her sister. Fourteen months later "the prince" arrived. Any slight affection Stephanie may have received from her father was directed at the apparent heir—her younger brother. Her heart was neglected and vulnerable. Three more siblings arrived by the time she was twelve, and

Stephanie's role as Mom #2 around the house was firmly established.

When she was sixteen, Jared, who sat next to her in her English class, began giving her the attention she had never received from her parents. Having been given no instruction from her parents about how to relate to a guy, she became confused when Jared's hands touched her in ways none ever had. Though she asked him to stop, the power of her thirst to be wanted by a male was overwhelming. It soon became clear to her that he desired her body much more than her heart. The power of being wanted overrode her self-restraint and self-respect. She battled to honor the goodness of her heart and made herself believe he really loved her. When she discovered that he had shown the pictures he took of her unclothed body to his friends on the basketball team, shame and self-hatred overwhelmed her. She had been mercilessly betrayed, but she believed she had caused it by yielding to her desire to be loved and cherished as a female.

Three months after her high school graduation, she gave birth to their first child and married Jared four months later. Since her heart had betrayed her, she would never allow herself to feel passion again. Her desires were dangerous, and so they were buried in a tightly sealed vault where no one would ever have access to them. Jared never learned to love her for the beauty of her heart but was content to grope her and get his sexual satisfaction by using a passionless woman. Stephanie would hide her body with loose-fitting clothing and dim her appearance with nondescript, asexual hair styles. To be a woman was to have a dangerous desire that would cause her to compromise herself, only to be used and humiliated. Her desire was her enemy.

Unsafe Desires

Your desires can be experienced as safe or unsafe. They can be welcomed as a positive force within you that will lead to deep satisfaction. The bride in Song of Solomon lived in joyous anticipation of being with her lover.

The stirrings within her heart were cultivated with images and fantasies of sexual encounters with her husband. Rather than moving away from her desires or in any way diminishing them, she reveled in them. Her desires were safe as she anticipated a loving, satisfying response to them.

Conversely, the desires of the heart may be feared as negative forces that lead to pain and emptiness. Abraham and his wife, Sarah, were a childless couple in a time when not having children was shameful. Some in the culture believed a childless couple had committed an offense that caused God to withhold the blessing of children from them. The painful ache for a child that tore up the insides of a barren wife and childless husband would have to be faced every time they even thought about children. So when the Lord visited Abraham and told him his wife would conceive a child, it was difficult for him to accept God's words. He resisted the hope and joy being offered. The desire for children was experienced as an ache for what could never be, and so it was unsafe. To hope was to hurt. Sarah laughed as a way of deflecting the hope that was coming alive in her heart.

We are talking about the Desiring Heart so you can clarify the God-given purposes within you that motivate almost all of what you do in relationship with your spouse. Our hope is that you may be able to discover or reclaim the thirsts that flow from your good or redeemed heart. But if you are in touch with your desires at all, you know you don't always embrace them as positive and good. Unlike the bride in Song of Solomon, your thirsts aren't freely embraced. Instead of being comfortable with them and delighting in them, you probably experience them as unsafe and are committed to managing them. We will clarify the good and bad heart later in the chapter. For now let's think about how you cope with the power of desires within the chambers of your heart. Your desires may be experienced negatively in one of three ways: deadened, dangerous, or desperate.

Deadened Desires

Picture the chambers in your soul as being lit by lights with drawstrings. When the string is pulled, the lights go on and the chamber is seen and is alive with color, sound, and power. However, when the string is pulled again, the lights go off and the depths of the chambers are darkened and hidden. As you think about entering into your chambers, envision the narrow entrance with its lights on. It is safe to let your heart be moved in the small, narrow entrance. But as the chamber widens, the lights are off and the depths are a place of dark mystery. Either the lights in them have been turned off or they were never on. Some people have never had the experience of being deeply cared for. No one has entered into their soul in such a way as to appropriately explore, appreciate, and enhance the richness of who they are. Their soul has been neglected. As a result the lights in their chambers are off, and their desires are deadened. No one is ever invited into a neglected person's heart. The lights exist but the strings have never been pulled. These people will say they don't need much.

Paul and Betsy

Paul grew up on a farm as the third of seven children. Work was hard on a dairy farm, with hours that started before dawn and ended after dusk. Paul's memories of his father were of a very tired man coming in from the barn around the time most of the family was going to bed. He would open the refrigerator, retrieve the plate of cold food his wife had dished, and either heat it in the oven or just eat it cold. Paul had little time for after-school activities and friends because he and his two brothers were expected to work the farm, something he had done for as long as he could remember. His parents quieted any dreams Paul may have had to pursue a career in the arts or sports. "The devil's distractions," he was told. No one had ever entered Paul's heart to explore with him the hopes and dreams latent in its chambers. As a hard worker and a dutiful son, he was useful to his family and did what was expected of him.

When the last of Paul and Betsy's three children had left their home,

Betsy was ready to begin the rest of her life. She wanted to run around the house naked and make love spontaneously with Paul. Having taken some short-term missions trips, her heart was tender toward the needy, and she desired to spend herself helping those with few resources. Paul wanted to work in the garage and watch television. He had little interest or energy for sex. The active life of a retiree had little appeal for him. He wished Betsy would settle down and stop being such a busybody. Betsy became depressed as she realized she may spend the rest of her life with a "dead man walking." Nothing moved Paul. Even when she told him that another man had become interested in her, and she was fighting temptation as she never had before, he allowed his heart to be unsettled for only a brief time. He quickly quieted the disturbance in the chambers of his heart and told Betsy that he knew she wasn't really serious about having an affair. Then he returned to his spot in front of the television and numbed himself by watching the history channel's rerun of the bombing of England during World War II. His heart was dead to desire.

Theresa

Rather than being neglected, many people have experienced someone entering into the deeper recesses of the chambers of their heart and doing damage. One woman, Theresa, told me that after her father died when she was five, her mother remarried within a year. Her stepfather was a gentle man who stepped up to the plate and assumed the role of a father in her life. Though she had already suffered a severe loss, she allowed him to turn on the lights in the deeper chambers of her heart. Her response to him was one of trust and admiration for his love and care. Their relationship grew and strengthened for several years.

The activity that bound them together was soccer. He was the coach for her premier club. When she was fourteen they traveled together to an out-of-state tournament. During one of the games she was troubled by back cramps, and he became concerned she would not be able to continue in the tournament. Between games, they returned to their hotel room. As father and daughter, they had become accustomed to rooming together when they traveled to a tournament. In the room, he suggested that he try to massage her back to help with the cramps, something he had done on many occasions. She had learned to relax with his therapeutic massages and enjoyed and trusted his fatherly care for her. Only this time the massaging became sensuous, and then it became sexual. Theresa had so deeply trusted her stepfather that she never saw it coming. When he abused her body as well as her trust, the sense of betrayal she felt was unspeakable. The drawstrings of the lights in her heart's chambers were pulled, the lights went off, and nothing but darkness remained. No man would ever be trusted to enter into her heart again. By the time she came to see me, her desire for any sort of intimacy with her husband was deadened to the point of numbness. In their ten years of marriage, she never allowed him to get close to her.

Dangerous Desires

Wounded or neglected people are sometimes able to manage their desires by deadening them. But others struggle to do this, fighting off cries of desire but having awareness that the chambers of their hearts are places of danger. They are dangerous because aliveness in the heart will either lead to being hurt again or tap into an appetite that is so powerful it could spin out of control. Many fear becoming alive so intensely that they will never allow anyone to care for them and access the chambers of their hearts.

Maggie and Wes

Maggie and Wes were in a very difficult marriage. Wes was cold and uncaring to Maggie. She learned to protect her heart by deadening desire and wanting little from him. She even dulled the heart pain she felt when she would see other men treat their spouses in a kind way. Tenderness and compassion had not been a part of her life for many years. What she thought was caring early in her marriage was actually a setup for being controlled and punished. She was terrified to hope that Wes could ever cherish her heart, since any kindness from him was just a trap for her to be hurt or rejected by him again. To open up to him was to set herself up to be crushed. Hope and vibrant desire were her enemies.

As God began getting Wes's attention concerning his anger and controlling ways, he started attending men's groups as well as engaging in individual counseling. He began to "get it" and developed an understanding of how harsh and punishing he had been to Maggie. God broke him, exposing his selfishness and arrogance and his heart became tender to his beloved. Romantic cards and special gifts replaced criticism and sarcasm. He became interested in her life and wanted to spend more time simply hanging out with her. Maggie's response to his change perplexed him. Instead of welcoming him into her life with warmth and aliveness, she shut him out even more. His kindness was met with coldness and a push away instead of an invitation in. Maggie's response to Wes troubled her as well, and even she wasn't sure why she became tougher and more distant as he became more loving. It wasn't so much that she didn't trust Wes or his motives as it was that she was terrified of herself. The desire to be loved was so powerful yet so intertwined with wounds that it was unsafe. Though deep within the chambers of her heart she wanted to be loved, she could not allow Wes's efforts to penetrate her and ignite her passion for love. If she did, her safe, controlled life would be disrupted, and the chaotic world of passion and pain would take over. Maggie would not permit herself to allow the lights to be turned on in the chambers of her heart. It was far easier to remain mistrustful and distant than it was to recognize and welcome the love he began to offer. Becoming alive was too dangerous and disruptive to her life.

Maggie had good reasons for protecting her heart. God designed Wes to be strong and to express his strength for the welfare of his wife, his beloved. But it seemed that when Maggie asked anything of him, he would become irritated and resent her requests. Hunting trips and sports were activities in his life that she could never challenge without risking his rage. He confessed to me that he did not understand why Maggie made him so angry and that he feared the depth of his rage against her. As with many angry men, the chambers of Wes's heart were entered by a needy, controlling mother.

His troubled mom used him to get her emotional needs met because his dad was distant and uncaring. His father had no clue how to address the cries of an angry, needy woman, so he gave his son the job. Complaints about how difficult her life was as a result of her pathetic, selfish husband would freely flow from his mother, who would often use her son as her confidant. As a sensitive son, Wes desired to make a difference and help her feel better, but inwardly he felt disgusted and drained by her ensnaring neediness. Of course, he experienced failure as his mother continued in her unhappiness despite his best efforts to help. The desire to be strong for a woman became associated with disgust and failure. So whenever Maggie asked anything of Wes, she turned on the lights in the chambers of his wounded masculine heart and exposed all the pain that was there as a result of his mother's exploitation. Rather than enjoying the experience of extending his strength for the welfare of his beloved, he felt violated and controlled. Wes was terrified to even talk about any of this because the rage that would come out of his heart could send out all sorts of danger signals. His desire to make a difference in a woman's life was dangerous because it elicited the corrupt passion for vengeance. Though he had never come close to being physically violent, Maggie told him she was continually afraid he would hurt her.

Desperate Desires

Our hearts have a way of refusing to be silenced. When a desire cannot be deadened and is not controlled by fear, it often compels a person to find satisfaction through desperate means. The pain of being unloved or seen as unacceptable can produce chaos within the chambers of the soul. Desires for justice get twisted with demands for satisfaction. The agony of feeling disrespected or unloved energizes a desperate demand to find fulfillment.

Ed and Jennifer

Jennifer, a mother of two young boys, came to counseling in order to find justification for the divorce she wanted. For twelve years she had endured the loneliness of a marriage where her husband, Eddy, spent a lot of time traveling and the rest of the time involved with church or some other activity. Though she voiced her complaints, she was always silenced with a guilt trip for being ungrateful for the opulent lifestyle his job provided. Ed was satisfied with accomplishments and recognition and had little desire to enter into Jennifer's world. Her desire for intimacy was neglected. She downplayed her attraction to television programs where lonely homemakers played out their fantasies with striking men. Jennifer thought she could control her desires and stay with Ed for the kids and because she had made a vow. Being a noble sufferer worked until Jeff noticed her suffering.

Jeff and his wife, Cindy, were friends of Jennifer and Eddy and were part of a couples' home group. One night after their group met, he asked Jennifer what was troubling her and if he could pray for her. The next week they met for coffee. His compassionate eyes gave her assurance she could pour her heart out to him concerning the emptiness of her marriage. Jeff's understanding and caring words pulled all the drawstrings on the lights in the chambers of her heart. She felt an aliveness and passion that had been dormant for over ten years. Once she tasted the power of the desires of her heart, she believed she could never go back to the emptiness and hypocrisy of her marriage to Eddy. It was out of moral integrity, she said, that she needed to divorce him. She could not silence the powerful cries of her heart that Jeff illumined and God ordained, or so she thought. Even if she believed it was wrong, her passion for Jeff was worth giving up everything, perhaps even her children. Where once she was dead, she had become alive. Fantasies can come true! Her desires were indeed desperate.

And then Jeff shared his heart. He described Cindy as being a mess. She was never satisfied with anything he did and let him know how unhappy she was with him. He did not feel she needed or wanted him for much more than being a handyman or babysitter. This dissatisfaction extended to the bedroom. Cindy did not find Jeff a very satisfying lover as she attacked him for being far more interested in the frequency of lovemaking as opposed to caring, prolonged expressions of love and eroticism. In other words, he wanted only "quickies" with her. Cindy's interest in sex waned while Jeff's did not. When she gave up trying to entice him to make love with her as opposed to using her for sex, he became desperate. His demand for sexual satisfaction would be gratified.

Pornography satisfied for a while, but his desperate heart wanted human touch. Sex phone lines and chat rooms mollified him but only deepened his desperation to master a woman by using her for sex. Jennifer and Jeff were vulnerable to each other's desires—both were souls desperate for satisfaction. In their reckless drive for satisfaction, they found themselves praying together, studying Scripture together, and feeling such a bonding of souls that they were able to justify having sex together. Strangely, as they felt they were meeting one another's emotional and spiritual needs, they sought ways to ease the pain for their spouses. Jeff felt Jennifer really needed him and that he made a profound difference in her life. She believed she had found her soul mate who made her feel special the way she had always longed for but never could with Eddy. Their desperate hearts deluded them into believing God so wanted them to be happy that he saw their actions as pure and holy instead of rash, selfish, and sinful.

GOOD HEART / BAD HEART —
GOOD DIRECTION / BAD DIRECTION

Let's take some time to make the complex simple. Our desires can come from a good heart or a bad heart. We can have a need that comes from a heart that is whole and good, or we can have a need that emerges from a heart that is corrupt and bad. The need may appear to be the same. The desire may not indicate whether it is from a good heart or a bad heart, or from good motives or bad motives. For example, we can desire to be respected for more than one reason. The desire for respect can come from a good heart or a bad heart. We can want to be respected for reasons that reflect God's design within us or for reasons that oppose his design. Sometimes it's a mixture of both, and we find a contradiction within our desires.

This contradiction within us leads to a mixed set of motives for almost every desire we experience. For instance I may desire to teach in my church. The agenda of my good heart is to be used of God and offer to others what he has taught me. The agenda of my bad heart is to be recognized by others and establish my own worth through what I do. These motives are present together. If I am not aware of both of them, the hidden motive will deceive me and fuel my desire. The hidden motive usually comes from my bad heart.

We are also capable of choosing good directions and bad directions. While it may seem that good directions always flow from a good heart, and bad directions come from a bad heart, it does not necessarily work that way. We can do right things for wrong reasons and wrong things for right reasons. We may be well-intentioned yet still choose a bad path. We may have dark motives lurking behind what appears to others to be a good path. Direction does not necessarily reveal the state of the heart.

Good Heart / Good Direction — Bad Heart / Good Direction

John and Carol were part of a couple's fellowship that included Jason and Alicia. The leader of their group had been encouraging the husbands to fulfill some of the romantic needs of their wives. He also emphasized that one of the ways a man shows leadership to his family is by his acts of service. The men, meeting on their own, decided to act upon what the group leader had suggested.

GOOD HEART / GOOD DIRECTION

John decided to take Carol away for a romantic weekend to a place she had been hinting she wanted to visit. He took her there because he cared about her and wanted to meet the needs of her heart. His choice to take her came from a good heart. The fact that he took her to a place she would enjoy reflected good direction.

BAD HEART / GOOD DIRECTION

Jason also decided to take his wife, Alicia, away for a romantic weekend to the same resort. Alicia had told him that one day she would like to go there for a weekend. His taking her there could be seen as a good action or a good direction. But Jason had an ulterior motive for taking her away that flowed from a selfish or corrupt heart. His agenda was to wine and dine her and then inform her that he had committed to spending a week golfing with his buddies at a different resort. This was an issue they had argued over, not arriving at an agreement. His taking her to a resort for a romantic weekend (good direction) was an attempt to manipulate her and prevent her from being angry that he made an irresponsible decision (bad heart).

GOOD HEART / BAD DIRECTION

Andrea, a salesperson who worked with John, was a widow with young children. When she expressed she was overwhelmed with home repairs, John felt moved to help her. He told Carol that he wanted to spend some time helping Andrea fix up her house. Carol expressed concern that he, a married man, would be alone in a home with a single woman. She knew John was a good man, that his desire to help came from a good heart, but she sensed a dangerous situation. She suggested that he not go alone but take some other men with him. John told her she had nothing to worry about. He wanted to follow the biblical mandate to help orphans and widows in their distress. He had a healthy desire flowing from a good, though naive, heart. His actions, working alone in a woman's home, proved to be a bad direction. Carol's intuition was right as Andrea, attracted by his caring nature, became possessive of John's time, causing friction between him and Carol. Eventually, realizing his wrong direction, he persuaded some other men to help her.

BAD HEART / BAD DIRECTION

Jason was faced with a similar situation when a divorcée, Deidra, who played on his softball team, told him she needed help figuring out her finances. Though Alicia voiced the same concerns as Carol had, Jason convinced her that his meetings with Deidra were only attempts to help her out: Alicia's concerns were groundless. He convinced her that he was doing what his small group leader had suggested and that his heart was good. But Jason had a selfish agenda flowing from a bad heart. He had guessed Deidra's real motive for getting together had nothing to do with finances, yet he wanted to meet with her anyway. Both his heart and his direction were bad.

Unless you know a person's heart, you will not know if his direction can be trusted as being good. If he is skilled, he can deceive you. If he doesn't know his own heart, he can easily deceive himself and believe his own deceptions. He can be a good-hearted fool or use good-looking behavior to disguise a selfish, bad heart.

You can see how seemingly good actions can cause confusion. Two people could do the same thing, but the action would flow from a good motive in one person and a wicked motive in the other. Or one person could do the same thing at different times and have different agendas. We are used to judging others on their behavior, but this framework forces us to look at the attitude of the heart toward the other person. *In making this choice, am I truly for my husband? In wanting this from my wife, is my heart good toward her, or am I seeking only to have my needs met?* Not only should your goal be to choose good, healthy actions, but it also needs to take into account the importance of your heart's position toward your beloved.

	GOOD HEART	BAD HEART
Good Direction	**Good Heart:** John's caring about Carol and wanting her to have a good time. **Good Direction:** Taking Carol for a weekend getaway.	**Bad Heart:** Jason's wanting to manipulate Alicia so she wouldn't be upset with him. **Good Direction:** Taking Alicia for a weekend getaway.
Bad Direction	**Good Heart:** John's wanting to help a widow in her distress. **Bad Direction:** Being alone with Andrea, putting him in a vulnerable position.	**Bad Heart:** Jason wanting to have a relationship with a divorced woman. **Bad Direction:** Being alone with Deidra, choosing to be in a compromising place.

CORRUPTED AND CONFUSED THIRSTS

Let's take the concept of good hearts and bad hearts and apply it to the longings expressed in the chambers of our hearts. How can you know if the desires you express are coming from a good place within you or if they have been corrupted by sin and by your encounters with a fallen world? The desires for relationship, purpose, and integrity may be attached to a healthy, redeemed heart, or they may spring from a selfish, corrupt heart. As a result, the way they are expressed may be in a manner that is destructive and leads to marital difficulties. This is why wisdom is needed to understand the motives of the heart. As we read in Proverbs, the wise man or woman studies his or her heart and allows others to expose the heart's agenda:

> The purpose in a man's heart is like deep water, but a man of understanding will draw it out. (Proverbs 20:5)

> Who can say, "I have made my heart pure; I am clean from my sin"? (Proverbs 20:9)

GODS AND SLAVES

Now let's take this understanding of good and bad hearts and see how it plays out in the purposes found in marriage for completion, enjoyment, and enhancement. We will also explore whether the direction of a desire is good or bad. When you are asked what you really want from your marriage and your spouse, the response from your *good heart* is that you desire to have a relationship that engages in the pursuits of completion, enjoyment, and enhancement. You must study each other as well as God's Word to understand how to move that desire in a *good direction*. "The heart is deceitful above all things, and desperately sick; who can understand it?" (Jeremiah 17:9).

However, since you wrestle with a fallen nature and live in a fallen world, everything you desire tends to also be influenced by a corrupted motivation coming from a *bad heart*. The corrupted motivation may set your desires in motion in a *bad direction*. Instead of viewing your spouse as an equal, joining with you for a mutual purpose, you view him in a self-serving way. You want him to be a *life source* who brings you ultimate satisfaction, or you desire him to be a *servant* who exists to meet your needs. In their extreme versions, the bad agendas bring you to view her as a *god* you worship or as a *slave* who must worship you and exists for your pleasure, giving you everything you require and having no rights of her own to ask anything from you.

These two distortions of godly desires share some characteristics but are significantly different. A life source is sought in order to establish well-being or, even deeper, healing and salvation. You may enter marriage with insecurity, with wounds, or without an identity. A life source provides healing, restoration, and identity. *"I know who I am and feel good about myself because of you. I am adequate or beautiful because you want me."* This is why many men are miserable if they are denied sex. As long as their wife agrees to have sex with them, all is well because their life source (goddess) has said, "you're the man" by agreeing to receive him sexually. They have an agenda for affirmation, not deep connection. We've seen wives treat their husbands horribly, but it's okay with them as long as the wives will have sex with them. Conversely, we have known women who will tolerate alcohol, pornography, name-calling, and more from their husbands, but who will believe everything is okay if their husbands (god) won't leave them. All is well because her life source is saying he won't leave.

While it makes sense to look to your spouse to complete you, your desire becomes corrupt when you look to him or her for salvation or redemption. Our parents modeled much of what is good in marriage. Dad came from an alcoholic family where love and nurture were unknown. Mom, orphaned young in life, had a giving and caring nature but was always an outsider in the family of her mother's sister, who took her in when she was two. Both our parents had significant health problems and suffered isolation and estrangement in their teen years. They had a depth of understanding and appreciation for each other's struggles. Though their health problems limited them, we never heard a single complaint about each other's physical limitations. Each was grateful to God for the blessings he gave them through each other. They completed each other in physical, emotional, and spiritual ways. The godly desires of our dad's heart, though, became corrupted as years went by. He began to see our mother as more than a soul mate; she became his source of life. She wasn't a colaborer who joined him as a helpmate through his journey of life; she was his life. His love for her may sound deeply romantic and admirable, but it actually became harmful to his soul as well as hers. While she lived, he felt strong. When she died, he felt like a shell of a man; nothing in life could touch him. When you see your spouse as your source of life, you are not satisfied with being completed by her. Instead you will begin to consume and possess her. You must have her, so you absorb her into your being.

The person who looks to a spouse for salvation often comes to marriage with deep wounds and insecurities. They become dependent upon their spouse to heal their wounds and provide relationship, meaning, and purpose. The energy that drives them isn't from a rich source within their spirit; it is from a fearful or wounded part of their soul. Their spouse must be a person who is powerful enough to heal them. So they will overlook their faults and idealize them, turning them into a god or goddess.

While you may desire a god to establish your well-being, you may also desire an admirer to enhance your identity. Your spouse is attracted to you because of the exceptional qualities you possess. She sees you as a physically attractive, smart, spiritual, or extraordinary person in many ways. She is appreciative and perhaps humbled that you find her attractive enough to marry. You have crafted a role for her and know exactly how she should live her life—especially how she needs to please and gratify you. In reality she is not a wife with mutual worth; she is more of a slave who exists to appreciate you and behave only in ways that please you. The slave is useful as a tool to help you express and enjoy yourself. Spouses in this situation are often seen as an extension of their wife or husband and have no identity of their own. *"You don't exist outside of my need for you."* A slave's value and worth are exploited for the gratification of the spouse.

In the next chapter we will more fully explore how dangerous spouses have taken the godly thirsts of a good heart and allowed them to be corrupted, resulting in a disastrous direction for their marriage.

CHAPTER 6

Dangerous Spouses

The good person out of the good treasure of his heart produces good,
and the evil person out of his evil treasure produces evil, for out of
the abundance of the heart his mouth speaks.
— Luke 6:45

And he did evil, for he did not set his heart to seek the LORD.
— 2 Chronicles 12:14

We expect divine joy from this human experience: that's why it ends
in such bitter disappointment. We have heaped on the shoulders of
the human beloved a burden of joy-making that only God can carry,
and we are scandalized when those shoulders break.
— Peter Kreeft, Heaven

What happens, then, if a corrupt heart fuels the desires for completion, enjoyment, and enhancement? We have seen that it is possible to take a healthy, godly thirst, twist and distort it, and end up with a dark agenda from a bad heart that drives us in a harmful direction. We want to journey through life with a partner who completes and fulfills us in ways that release us from our loneliness and isolation and who moves us toward all we can become in Christ. To be one with a beloved, to be known and found to be of great value provides substantial meaning and worth to our being. We do not feel entirely whole without such a relationship. The spouse who provides such a relationship cannot be an ordinary person. No, we think of such a mate as one with unique and almost mystical powers to love and live. While we can enjoy being loved by an extraordinary lover, the danger comes when we grant our spouse a status beyond that of a human, or when our spouse assumes a status that puts him or her in the place of God.

If we allow ourselves to enter the deepest areas in the chambers of our hearts we will discover the truth Christ knew all too well: The strongest longings of our soul are for internal purity and eternal connection. We seek relationship with one capable of offering us healing from the internal and external wounds of living in a fallen world. A voice within us groans from the deepest part of our being with a desire for wholeness. Being able to connect with the source of this wholeness, the granter of life, becomes essential to our ongoing existence. However, when a good thing becomes an ultimate thing, the realm of danger has been entered. When we confuse the beauty of what is available in our marriage with the majesty that is available only in God, we burden our relationship with far more significance than it can bear.

Rather than appropriately enjoying and enhancing our spouse, we wrongly use them as a means to integrate with the Eternal Giver of Life. The faulty structure of our marriage will finally implode under the weight of such a burden. When it does, our relationship will fracture, and our spouse will pay the price for being unable to provide life to us. So if we don't see that we have followed a bad direction by deifying our husband or wife, we will feel justified for punishing our spouse for being unable to give us the life that in reality only God can provide.

MARRIAGE TO A DANGEROUS SPOUSE

Most people who are married to dangerous spouses don't realize it. That sounds crazy, doesn't it? "Crazy" is how many people who are

married to such a spouse feel. Oh, they may know their spouse is difficult and, occasionally, destructive. They would agree that something is
very wrong. But dangerous? Or worse, evil? To admit who their spouse
really is could bring their world crashing down, shattering every hope
within them. So they live in denial, always praying and hoping they can
find the one thing that will bring out the good side of their spouse.

This is understandable because no one is all good or all bad. Even
dangerous and destructive spouses will occasionally offer kindness and
care—a tease for what their spouse thinks is fully available in them.
And sometimes a caring spouse can see the healthy desires buried
underneath the corrupted heart. The good heart wants to believe love
and intimacy can be found in the dangerous spouse. Their souls have
been designed to hope. Accepting the truth about their husband or wife
brings them into the empty cavern of despair and darkness. The impli-
cations for their future are devastating. It's easier to pretend.

As we stated, many people married to dangerous persons are filled
with confusion and turmoil. Remember, dangerous spouses will take
no responsibility for their relational destructiveness. In fact, the way
they treat their partner makes sense to them. Unfortunately, many
people bring wounds from the past into their marriages and are numb
to the pain of mistreatment, having had to find ways to normalize and
survive it in other relationships. It may even make sense to them that
they are mistreated. Someone trying to find the goodness and logic in
the way a dangerous spouse relates has about as much chance of suc-
ceeding as someone who tries to explain the sensibilities of a terrorist.
The dangerous spouse is usually all too ready to blame the partner for
the problems in the marriage. Hopeful but naive partners are often far
too willing to accept the blame.

Another reason someone with a dangerous spouse doesn't want to
accept reality is shame. *"How could I not have seen it?"* *"I can't believe I
was so foolish to have made such a disastrous choice. What have I done to
my children?"* *"I guess my parents and friends were right when they warned
me not to marry him or her. I feel like such a fool."* These are the voices of

the Enemy. God is a God of truth. Strength is available in him to face your worst nightmares. Freedom is available only if you are courageous enough to face the truth.

Let's take a deeper look at how healthy patterns of completion, enjoyment, and enhancement can be distorted by two dangerous spouses: *the consuming spouse* and *the exploiting spouse.* We will explore each one's makeup as the pieces begin to fit together when the character of a dangerous spouse is clarified, understood, and accepted.

The Consuming Spouse

> And he received the gold from their hand and fashioned it with a graving tool and made a golden calf. And they said, "These are your gods, O Israel, who brought you up out of the land of Egypt!" (Exodus 32:4)

Exodus 32 relates the tragic story of the Hebrew people turning away from God and making an idol for their own worship. Even Aaron, Moses' brother who had been one of the seventy-four who had seen God (see Exodus 24:9-10), encouraged the making of a golden calf as a substitute for God and publicly proclaimed a day of feasting and worship. Ironically, while this was happening, God was giving Moses a covenant that would instruct men and women how to engage with God as the true source of life.

This passage is packed with spiritual and theological riches. One of the truths that emerges from it is that we are unable to tolerate incompleteness for very long. Moses was gone only forty days before the people demanded a god to worship. A second truth is that we will use a godly thirst to take a good thing, meant to be utilized and enjoyed, and turn it into an ultimate thing to be worshipped. The gold and jewelry the Hebrew people wore and possessed was a good thing, provided by God for enjoyment as well as function. But the Hebrew people tried to satisfy their godly desire by turning the gold into an ultimate thing—a life-giving god. A third truth this story yields is that we are so simple, or foolish, that we may believe the god we have made is actually worthy of worship and our source of life. Despite the knowledge that they had crafted the bull with their own hands, the Hebrew people believed it to be worthy of their worship, having lost sight of the glory of the incomparable, true God. Finally, when we have made our own god, we, as the Hebrew people, can justify any sort of behavior we wish. One distortion of truth led to more as they turned worship into an orgy of self-indulgence. It is possible to turn our spouse into our god and justify selfishness.

Derrick and Erica

Erica was mildly amused when her church announced it was holding a conference for troubled marriages. Marital stresses and strains were hard to imagine when you were married to someone like Derrick. He was a man who knew how to care for a woman. Always understanding, Derrick devoted himself to her and their marriage. They really appeared to be "one" in their church. Youth leaders, abstinence teachers, and all around servants, they were a model couple.

Derrick and Erica were inseparable. He was always wrapped around her, emotionally as well as physically. Some wondered if his frequent touching her evidenced a bit of clinginess. Yet Erica thought if the church ever wanted a man to teach other men how to care for their wives, Derrick was the man. She knew this because she was his soul mate and his queen, and he was selflessly devoted to her.

Not all of Erica's friends saw Derrick the way she did. Some were concerned that she always had to check in with him when they were planning things. Didn't she ever get tired of being so nice? They thought she dressed modestly to a fault, largely because Eric was critical of her when she tried to "compete" with other women. Several of her friends felt Derrick put tons of pressure on her to be the perfect Christian wife. Was she ever allowed to refuse him sexually? Could she say no when he signed up for yet another volunteer commitment? There just seemed to be something artificial or inauthentic about the way they related.

Yet her friends couldn't clearly identify what it was that didn't seem genuine about the marriage. Still, they thought Erica and Derrick were good and caring people. "Dangerous" would not have been the way they described either of them.

One fall, Erica's friends decided to attend an intriguing retreat that focused on exploring and offering God's resources for healing the pain in souls wounded by abuse and loss. They felt they nearly had to twist truth to convince her to join them for the weekend. Since Derrick suspected the speaker and topic were not on the list of "doctrinally correct" presenters and subjects, he was skeptical. Besides, why would someone who was so godly, so mature, need to be healed inside? He was more than happy to have her attend seminars on discipleship and mentoring, but inner healing made no sense to him. Erica's friends went through the back door and suggested that it would be beneficial for her to attend so she might be able to help other women who had inner wounds. Derrick reluctantly allowed her to go.

Derrick was a bit nervous as he thought of Erica at the seminar. He wondered why she would even be interested in going to "that type" of weekend. She was an incredible woman. There was absolutely nothing in her that needed to be fixed. Still, he had a confidence he could poke holes in any notions the workshop might put into her head leading her to think otherwise. That's where he was wrong.

When Erica arrived home from the weekend, two of her friends helped her into the living room of her house. Derrick was startled to see the tears and troubled look on her face. He grew increasingly uncomfortable when she said it had been the second most painful weekend of her life. She needed to tell him something and wanted her friends to stay while she opened her heart to him. Derrick felt a flash of anger come up within him. What had they done to her? He knew she should never have gone to some wacky woman's weekend. And why did she need her friends there? No couple had ever been more open and honest than they were with one another. Didn't she trust him? Inside his heart, he was terrified she may have changed.

"Honey, I haven't been truthful. I am so sorry. You think I'm such a wonderful, godly person, but I'm not who you think I am." Erica then related the painful story of a high school romance that went very bad. The most painful weekend she had ever experienced occurred years ago and was spent alone, with the sights, sounds, and smells of an abortion clinic assaulting any shred of dignity she felt within her. For over twenty years she had been carrying the tortuous memory of the baby she aborted. "I am so sorry," she said. "I know I told you I had never been with anyone else. I thought I could just put my pain away in a dark room and give all my care to you. But the awareness of what I did, the child I lost, and the lie you have believed have tormented my soul. I can't do it anymore. I need—we need—to be free from the deception. I knew we could never be as close as God wanted if I continued to allow you to see me as someone I never was. But now that you know the truth—I know this is strange—for the first time I feel hope. And I feel like I really want you to know me, the real me."

Erica finished and looked at Derrick with eyes he had never seen before. Her eyes were filled with anguish, hope, and a deep desire that he would rush to her, embrace her, and love her in a way not possible before. Derrick walked over to her, hugged her, and told her it was all right. Everything would be okay. And then he left.

Derrick's life would never be the same. His goddess had died. He was alone. But more so, he felt an enormous sense of betrayal. Rage existed side by side with despair. How could she have done this to him when he had believed in her and trusted her so deeply? He felt as lost as he did when his parents sat him and his brother down in their living room to tell them of their impending divorce. Once again all he had believed in and hoped for was gone in a sixty-second disclosure.

For years after his parents' announcement, loneliness and vacancy of spirit characterized Derrick's being. Then he met Erica. The first time he saw her he knew she was perfect. Everything about her spoke of goodness and purity. She was different. He knew she was "the one." In her presence he found rest, peace, and wholeness. She completed him like no other ever had. And he wanted her. He wanted *all* of her, or so he thought. What was attractive to him were the parts of her that fulfilled his fantasy of a pristine maiden who could heal his soul from the darkness of his unrest. The rest of her, especially the messy parts, was rejected by him. Her desire to wrestle with life and God were trivialized by both of them.

Initially Erica was confused by his adulation. It felt wonderful to be so valued, even if she didn't understand all he saw in her and why he thought she was *that* special. She felt a compassion for Derrick as she heard about his wounds from his parents' divorce and his sense of alienation from his father. One thing she knew: She would never disappoint him or betray his confidence the way others had. Plus, Derrick was a good guy with whom she could craft a future.

Couples heal each other. We can address many of the wounds life has perpetrated on our spouse, and our beloved can do the same for us. This is a good thing: It is inherent in the process of becoming one flesh. But problems start when a good thing becomes an ultimate thing. No human can satisfy the deepest longings of our hearts. No husband or wife can redeem our fallen and wounded soul. If we are honest, no one can love us as powerfully as our hearts desire.

Derrick had come to believe that Erica was his salvation. Oh, he knew better. He really was a good man who understood that his wife was human and had imperfections. It even became clear to him that he was replaying his father's betrayal through Erica's disclosure. The frightened and confused high school girl committed no offense against him. But in the deeper regions of his soul, where the chaotic and inarticulate passions scream, he desperately demanded she save him. So Erica was never free to be less than wonderful. This was why she could never tell him about the abortion. She knew he wanted her to be a pure, virginal source of love that he could possess for his own healing.

It was only after she told him about the abortion that she began to realize that she had been consumed by Derrick throughout their marriage. He hadn't married her; he married an ideal who would make his life work for him. It wasn't Erica he wanted to complete him; it was a virginal essence who was incapable of betrayal or criticism. The core of her beauty would never be pursued. As long as she played the role assigned her, life was very nice. Not profound or exhilarating, but pleasant. Erica realized that she had often felt somewhat like a child around him. Life was happy and safe but uninspiring.

Conversely, she also felt like a mother making it "all better" for her little boy. She really wasn't so innocent and pure, but Derrick couldn't handle her spicier side. As the truth in how they related became apparent, she began resenting his controlling and pouty ways. She now understood why she was so uncomfortable being introduced as his "incredible wife." She wasn't incredible; she was Erica. The fact was that she could never have differing ideas that would challenge him because they would only expose his insecurities. He had loved her from his weakness, not strength. And she started despising his weakness. But her real sadness came from an awareness that she couldn't retrieve the lost years. She wondered what life would have been like with a husband who desired her to complete him with the depth of who she was instead of who he compelled her to be.

Some men and women in this situation work through the difficulties and, in a wonderful way, are able to restructure their marriages and their lives. And some don't do this. Derrick did not. He refused her call to a mature love between two fallen lovers. A union that required grace, soul-level forgiveness, and a call to holiness would require too much of him. He remained content in his growing bitterness. He never forgave her for the abortion and, instead, began to think of her as a "slut" or "damaged goods," even referring to her this way in public. How could she betray him the way she did? While they never divorced, he found ways to make her pay. He would never recognize that he was unwilling to do the hard work of reconstructing their marriage based on truth. Because the truth was that he was a dangerous spouse—he was willing to strip Erica of her dignity in order to convince her that her role in life was to be his salvation. Erica's truth was that she was willing to withhold her real heart in order to get the security and peace of a worshipping spouse. Sadly, only Erica was willing to change. She was willing to allow God to forgive her, heal her, and transform her into someone who was able to do the mature work that would lead to soul-to-soul completion. The clarifying and cleansing took time but resulted in a thriving soul. Tragically, she would live the rest of her life with a man who would never embrace the beauty of the woman she really was and would despise her for not being his savior. In his eyes she only pretended to be his beloved, and instead of loving him she had made a fool of him. He never allowed himself to experience the true thirst for deep relationship and love. Settling for the pain of a betrayed child, his soul existed in darkness and torment. Though he longed for wholeness, he settled for the power of bitterness.

The Exploiting Spouse

We have seen how the healthy desire to complete and be completed can turn into a destructive dynamic in a marriage. A spouse who desires completion can consume the mate and resent him or her for not being a god. Conversely, the spouse who accepts the role of being a savior will eventually break. Now we will look at how the rich passion for mutual enjoyment and enhancement within a marriage can be corrupted by another dangerous spouse, the exploiter.

In 2 Samuel 11, Scripture tells the story of David and Bathsheba. A vivid description of an exploiter can be found in this passage. One night David got out of his bed and went to his roof, apparently to check out the scenery. He saw a married woman and a father's daughter, Bathsheba, bathing and decided to exploit her physical beauty for his own pleasure. After he was finished, he sent her on her way, probably thinking nothing about his utter selfishness. When he was told that she got pregnant from his self-gratification, he was only able to see her pregnancy in light of how it would affect him. He wouldn't be able to keep his reputation as a godly leader and a great warrior if word got out that he impregnated the wife of one of his noble soldiers, Uriah, who was at war fighting for the nation. He brought Uriah home and tried to get him to have sex with Bathsheba so he would think he got Bathsheba pregnant, keeping David's "dignity" and image intact.

Uriah would not allow himself to have marital pleasure because he felt it would be unjust to do so while the other soldiers slept in tents in open fields, guarding the ark. Instead of being shamed by Uriah's nobility, David remained concerned about his own reputation. He decided to have Uriah killed by sending him and his troops to the dangerous front lines of the battles. Apparently David had no guilt in justifying destroying the lives of his noble soldiers and taking the life of a powerless woman's husband. It was all about him. Everyone existed to enhance his well-being. A person's heart, pain, or even life meant nothing to him if it interfered with what mattered to him.

David saw what he wanted and apparently believed he was entitled to have it. He took what he desired with no regard for the consequences of his behavior upon Bathsheba and others. She mattered to him only as far as she was useful to him. Bathsheba, a married woman, existed for David's pleasure and nothing more. While we don't know the condition of Bathsheba's heart, whether she had a dark heart that welcomed David's attention or whether she had a good heart but was powerless to refuse him, we can surmise King David never did the work to discover the beautiful soul within her. If he had allowed himself to explore a noble thirst within him, he never could have allowed himself to exploit her physical and sensual beauty while disregarding her soul. Not until God exposed David through Nathan did David consider his own selfishness and evil.

God tells of the horrible destruction that resulted from David's exploitation. Uriah was murdered, many men died, and the child born from David's selfishness also died. One can only speculate about the damage done to the soul of Bathsheba as she lost her husband and her child and was publicly stripped of her dignity. The respect among the Hebrew people for God's anointed king must have diminished greatly. Only God's gracious mercy to David allowed him to be transformed and redeemed.

Ian and Judy

Judy's first marriage was to a highly successful man who, much like her father, was a man for all seasons. Aaron seemingly could accomplish anything, from doing home repairs to excelling at sports to making piles of money. But unlike her father, he never had enough time for her. Plus, he was more interested in his toys and politics than he was with his wife. Judy felt cheated and betrayed by Aaron. After all, she had incredible taste, was smarter than most of the people she knew, and had plenty of men who couldn't take their eyes off her. She never understood why he had several affairs.

Tired of being ignored by Aaron, she eventually divorced him and quickly found Ian, a gym teacher and wrestling coach at her son's junior high. Ian came from a blue-collar family, was modestly accomplished, and had simple tastes. He was a good guy who loved his motorcycle and was not a man who would ever betray anyone. She was drawn to Ian because he had potential. He was a good-looking guy who needed to be cleaned up a bit, but he was a bright man who was well respected in their church and community.

Ian was fascinated with Judy. She was more interesting than any woman he had ever met. She could talk about politics, religion, and even sports—especially wrestling. He certainly didn't think he was on her level, but she made him feel like he was the most stimulating man she had ever met, at least in the beginning of their relationship. Being on the shy side, Ian was a bit uncomfortable being around Judy and all the attention she seemed to draw. A people person, she was always surrounded by an attentive crowd admiring her latest outfit or creative idea. One thing that always irritated him was why she felt a need to coach him on how to dress and what to say around her friends. It hadn't occurred to him that his dress and speech were substandard. Yet he felt special being around her and never wanted to lose her, so he kept his annoyance with her criticisms to himself.

After they had been married for a while, Judy decided they should sell his small three-bedroom home and buy a large, old Victorian mansion—a fixer-upper so they could entertain more. Though he didn't quite understand why she insisted on such a large house, he was getting used to accommodating her. His style of clothing had changed as well as his taste in music. He learned to stop talking so much about God after Judy told him his God talk was embarrassing her in front of her friends. She didn't want to hang out much with his motorcycle buddies, and his family bored her, so they spent less and less time with the people who had been close to him.

Ian wanted to satisfy Judy so he agreed to buy the home and redo the place. He was unaware that her exploitive demands would never be satisfied—he would never be enough for her, and he would not be able to remodel the house in a way that would meet her standards. But he would try.

In his attempt to please her, he dedicated himself to renovating the house in his spare time. Judy's idea was that any time outside of teaching and coaching was spare time. Spare time was her time. She deserved a beautiful home, and so she never considered he would want to do anything other than spend all his energy doing what she wanted. Judy insisted each weekend be a house repair marathon. She was furious if he dared to relax or take a break to be with friends. God forbid he would take time to go to a coach's clinic. When Ian tried to do something for himself, she would tell him how selfish he was and how much it hurt her that he didn't care enough about her to follow through with his promise to renovate the house. The tension between trying to satisfy her while addressing some of his own needs caused turmoil and confusion in his heart. He was never at peace.

Working on the home led to increasing conflict within their marriage. Ian tried to be prudent with their finances, but he had to balance financial integrity against Judy's demands. Her assertion was that if she was going to be in a Victorian mansion, it had to look like one. If he didn't have the money to pay for it, Daddy would. The message she sent was clear: "Don't embarrass me by doing sloppy work with cheap material." Inside his heart, he felt defeated. He knew she was right. Besides, she only wanted a nice home. He was certain that Aaron or her dad could have done a great job on the house. Plus, they wouldn't have to worry about how much everything cost. It made no sense to him why someone like her would settle for a guy like him who just didn't have what it takes. He had no clue what to do with his resentment and growing irritation toward her.

Ian began to understand that his value to her was what he could do for her. Who he really was disinterested her. Motorcycles and wrestling were referred to as activities for Neanderthals. She told him he was shallow because he didn't enjoy reading books on spiritual growth and gender issues and never really engaged her in discussions on these matters. The contempt he felt from her diminished him. But he knew his job was to serve his spouse as Christ served the church. Weariness of body and spirit was ever present, resulting in a weight that began to break him.

After one weekend when he spent more than twenty-five hours putting tiles in a foyer, she ripped into him in front of some friends for the poor job she said he had done. As the assaults continued, his depression, self-doubt, and rage grew. Her contempt for his modest craftsmanship and his lack of funds grew into open expressions of mockery. By the time he gave up and put the house up for sale, he had lost contact with friends and had withdrawn into television and the Internet, sullen and beaten. When she divorced him, she made it clear to all her friends that he was to blame because he wasn't man enough to deal with her and keep his promise to provide a home for her. He was willing to accept the blame for the marital failure. Her friends heard her deride him for not having the strength to say no to her. It wasn't long before she moved on to her next admirer. He never remarried.

Exploiting spouses enjoy and enhance for their own pleasure with no regard for the well-being of their mates. They are gods and goddesses who "deserve" to be served. Their spouses are simply extensions of them — they don't exist outside of the exploiters' need for them. Exploiters find their husbands or wives useful to them. A husband often feels like a "paycheck," and a wife experiences herself as an "escort" or a "body for his pleasure." True mutual enjoyment and enhancement never occurs because that sort of intimacy and love requires profound respect for the well-being and sensibilities of the spouse. Ian was valued because he was useful to Judy. When he couldn't come through for her on her terms, he had outlived his usefulness and was discarded. The exploiter demands that her spouse acts and thinks in ways that please her. She feels perfectly free to criticize and correct anything she dislikes or disagrees with. Body size, sexual functioning, ways of parenting, recreational preferences, family, diet, beliefs, and much more are fair game for the exploiter to pass judgment on. The exploiter has a sense of superiority and is always right.

One major problem in being married to an exploiter is that typically no one but the spouse knows who he or she really is. Often they are seen as caring and charming individuals. This is how exploiters begin a relationship. They are charismatic and munificent, making their future spouses feel more special and wonderful than they ever imagined they could. The exploiter is often able to demonstrate what an amazing husband or wife he or she is. And in their core, they really believe they are brilliant. Their spouse is the one who simply doesn't get it. An unrepentant exploiter lacks the capacity to reflect on his or her selfishness. Remember, it took a direct act of God to break David and get him to recognize his narcissism and sin. The highest need exploiters allow themselves to have is *admiration*. They crave admiration while not understanding they are unable to accept or even ask for love because love would allow them to be flawed and human, and that is the very thing they fear.

Sometimes an exploiter is perceived as a suffering person married to an uncaring or irresponsible spouse. Judy was able to garner much sympathy for herself. After all, she had helped Ian out so much, and look what she got in return. No one knew that she believed she was entitled to treat Ian any way she wanted because he was lucky to have her. Like David with Bathsheba, Judy assumed Ian should feel privileged to be used by her.

OTHER DANGEROUS SPOUSES

The Punishing Spouse

"The first time he called me a b**** was on our wedding day. I was unhappy that the caterer dropped the top tier of the wedding cake. I was polite to the caterer but clearly upset. He called me a b**** in front of the entire wedding party and my parents. He has called me that word at least once a week for the past fifteen years. Despite five years of counseling, he has never stopped the verbal assaults. And each time he says it, it is like I've been punched in the stomach. I never get used to it. My kids just look at me with pity. I'm his wife. I try to love him as well as I can. I feel like there is not much of me left."

Punishing spouses hurt their mates. A woman told me how her husband would regularly start picking a little fight with her early in the evening. The fight would continue until the kids went to bed, and then it would escalate until one or two o'clock in the morning. He would bully, demean, and punish her until she was huddled in the corner in tears, begging him to stop. It wasn't until he thoroughly defeated her that he would back off; after using her for his sexual pleasure, he would fall contentedly asleep, leaving her in agony. The next morning he would wake her and demand breakfast, as he happily prepared to leave for his job as an executive in a major corporation, where he was known as a "fantastic guy." Sadly, he was looked up to as a leader in his church. No one ever believed her when she tried to tell her story. To this day, he has never repented for his years of violating his wife's soul with his hatred and fear of women.

The *punisher* is typically one who does not know how to receive love and out of his (or her) insecurities, wounds, or evil nature rejects love and acts on a dark desire for *harm* or *revenge*. The punisher may or may not express strong emotions, may be direct or indirect, but will find a way to inflict pain. They are so reckless and selfish that they often enjoy the pain they cause.

One way to understand the core drive in punishing spouses is that they have a deep fear of being mastered or controlled by the opposite sex, so their attacks are intended to emasculate or pound their spouses into submission. A man will never enjoy his masculinity in the presence of a punishing wife, and a woman will never feel safe or appreciated as a woman if she is married to a punishing husband. They assault their spouses in order to cut down or punish their expressions of manhood or womanhood. Their true heart of desire is buried under the tyranny of their rage and fear. They will never enjoy the depth of love God designed for them. Instead, they will allow expressions of power to satisfy them.

The Demeaning Spouse

When I was in high school, I remember having dinner with some other guys at a friend's house. We were seated around a large table when his mother began serving food to all of us. His father entered the room after having used the bathroom. As soon as he sat down at the table, his wife shot at him, "Did you wash your hands after touching that filthy thing?" Needless to say we were stunned, and he was completely humiliated in front of this group of teenage boys. What was interesting was that he said nothing, put his napkin on his lap, and began to eat his dinner. What could he do or say? *Her attack left him no room for a reasonable response.* He could rip into her and start a brawl in front of everyone, or he could walk out of the room with his dignity shredded. Her contempt for him was clearly evident.

While her comments could be seen as punishing, the greater effect was to demean or humiliate him. Demeaning is almost always done in front of an audience, while punishing is usually done in secret. I remember this man as an accomplished construction worker who loved his truck and tools. I doubt that she ever appreciated his strength as a man but rather was relentless in faultfinding and diminishing any expression of masculinity he offered. She was dangerous to his manhood. What she didn't understand was that by demeaning and repelling him, her soul would never be entered by a loving man. Sadly, her God-given beauty would never be expressed, seen, or enjoyed. I wonder if he ever wept for her barren soul.

"What did you do all day? The place is a mess! What do you mean, 'dinner isn't ready yet'?" John raged at Sara as soon as he walked in the door. The kids were in earshot, taking in the grand assault on their mom. John had no hesitation when it came to letting Sara know what a failure she was to him. Nothing she did was right. His attacks and patronizing comments let her know she was despised by her husband. His private comments about her weight and lack of sexual desire ripped her heart. His public use of profanity demeaned her.

Once, when she went away for the weekend to visit her ailing mother, he decided to show her that her life wasn't so bad. When she arrived home, all the clothes were washed, folded, and put away. The house was completely cleaned up, including a radical cleaning of the kitchen and bathrooms. He had made all the meals for the family from scratch. Oh yes, he made sure the kids told her he had taken them to the park. His smug smile told her of his immense disrespect for her as a woman. Even he, a man, could be a better mother and homemaker than she could. Sara would never experience being prized and enjoyed in the presence of her dangerous husband. John was unable to understand that by demeaning his beloved he was driving away any chance of ever knowing love.

The Raging Spouse

While the punisher has many ways to inflict harm, the *rager* does it by attacking with murderous emotions. Raging spouses use anger and force to intimidate, punish, and control their spouse. The ragers can be males or females. The key characteristic is that they carry an ominous air behind everything they say or do. One never knows when the rager will launch with an explosion intended to annihilate a spouse. A seemingly wonderful evening can be turned into a war zone by the unpredictable eruption of the rager. Many who are living with a rager have the experience of having to walk on eggshells so they don't trigger an explosion from their spouse. Of course, the rager typically feels fully justified for his or her destructiveness and has no sympathy for the spouse bearing the trauma he or she has inflicted. Often, if the rager is not violent, the spouse wishes he or she would become physically aggressive as the pain from physical abuse seems less to the victim than that experienced from an emotional rage episode.

Dave (from the "Dave and Patty" section in chapter 1) was a rager. The car ride home from any gathering was a place where he would launch his venomous attack. "I can't believe you told them about the mess in our basement. What the h*** is wrong with you? Don't you have any brains at all?" As he slammed the steering wheel, he continued the attack, oblivious of the kids sitting in frightened silence in the backseat. "I have told you a million times that I don't want anyone to know my business! Why did you do that? Answer me. Don't sit there with your head up your butt!"

Of course, Patty had no way of stopping the tirade. She was powerless to influence him in any way at all. A rager is a proverbial fool who is unable to receive input. She typically had panic attacks whenever he launched an assault. When he was finished with his explosive episode, he would threaten to rage again if she wouldn't kiss and make up.

The rager is a bully who intimidates his or her spouse. It is not unusual for a spouse of a rager to develop physical illnesses as well as depression and anxiety from having to cope with the destructiveness of the angry spouse. An additional stress for the spouse is when the children are living under the same threat of a destructive tirade. As with the exploiter, friends and family may never see the dark, punishing side of a rager. Instead, they may think the rager is a warm, wonderful husband or wife. To complicate matters, the spouse is often afraid to tell anyone about the rage. The husbands or wives fear that either they won't be believed or the rager will find out and make them pay.

We realize these examples appear to be extreme, and those with non-difficult spouses must think that few people really have dangerous spouses. But please understand that many good, godly people have dangerous spouses who have caused them to question their sanity and worth. By clearly accepting a spouse as dangerous, a person has a reference point to clarify and understand the damaging behaviors of the husband or wife. If you are married to a dangerous spouse, you must find a way to shield yourself from his or her destructive words and behaviors. Proverbs 4 instructs us to guard our hearts because they are vulnerable to all sorts of evil, especially a dangerous spouse.

At this point many marriage books might describe how marital technology and prayer radically changed the difficult spouses we have described. They learned how selfish they were and how much pain they caused their spouses. A selfish, corrupt heart was broken and transformed into a loving, tender life-giving source. It happens. And it doesn't happen. Some spouses don't change. Authentic, loving, one-flesh intimacy will never be experienced with an unchanging, difficult spouse. Yet there is hope. Much hope.

PART 3

When It All Goes Wrong

COMING TO GRIPS WITH THE LOSS

CHAPTER 7

The Wounded Heart

My tears have been my food day and night, while they say to me all the day long, "Where is your God?" These things I remember, as I pour out my soul: how I would go with the throng and lead them in procession to the house of God with glad shouts and songs of praise, a multitude keeping festival. Why are you cast down, O my soul, and why are you in turmoil within me? Hope in God; for I shall again praise him, my salvation.

— *Psalm 42:3-5*

Laments of the Wounded Heart

The ache of loneliness is unbearable. I groan in places nothing can touch.

The evidence of my failures is written all over my spouse.

Do you know what it's like to lie next to your beloved in a darkened bedroom, to long to be touched, and to have your spouse recoil in cold disgust if your bodies happen to merely brush together?

How little they know of the grief of silent nights.

When I looked in his eyes and saw how much he loathes me, it felt like my soul died.

I just want to be loved; is that so bad?

No one knows the ways she has methodically destroyed any sense of worth I once had.

Do you know what it's like to lie next to your spouse in a darkened bedroom, dreading the moment when your bodies touch and your flesh experiences yet another violation?

I live every day knowing that my spouse wishes I were dead.

He has never understood me. I just realized that he has never known who I really am.

THE WOUNDED HEART

Definition: A wounded heart is one that has been damaged by assault, neglect, or abandonment. The wounds limit the heart's capacity to enjoy full expression in giving and receiving. Shame, fear, or bitterness replaces joy within its chambers.

If the design of your heart is to experience joy in the sharing and expression of its chambers, wounds limit or distort that experience. Recognizing your wounds and eventually clarifying and reclaiming uncorrupted desires is a large part of "thriving despite." We want to clarify the types of wounds your heart may carry as well as the desires behind those wounds. What you'll discover is that throughout life your desires and wounds have interacted in such a way that you may fear your desires and distort your wounds, not seeing them clearly.

CANDOR — DO YOU HAVE THE COURAGE TO
TAKE AN HONEST LOOK?

Biblical Candor: Candor is courageous truth telling about life to myself in which I come face-to-face with the reality of internal and external suffering.[1]

We are often taught to deny reality and minimize pain with sayings such as "Stop having a pity party," "Just trust God and everything will be okay," "You know he didn't really mean to hurt you," or "At least she isn't going to leave you." No oncologist would tell a woman to ignore ominous lumps in her breast or overlook excessive bleeding. Pretending that drinking twelve beers a day is harmless doesn't protect the liver from being destroyed by alcohol. So why would we think that just saying relational pain doesn't hurt can prevent the soul from being wounded and scarred?

> *I mislabeled things. I'm a master at not seeing what's obvious in front of me. I wouldn't see them as they really are because to see the truth is too painful. To see evil in my spouse is devastating because it crushes the hope that I will ever know the love I thirst for. To see the evil in me . . .*
> *—A client, coming into awareness of wounds*

God doesn't ignore relational problems and is swift to acknowledge all of reality, especially mankind's offenses.

The LORD saw that the wickedness of man was great in the earth, and that every intention of the thoughts of his heart was only evil continually. And the LORD was sorry that he had made man on the earth, and it grieved him to his heart. So the LORD said, "I will blot out man whom I have created from the face of the land, man and animals and creeping things and birds of the heavens, for I am sorry that I have made them." (Genesis 6:5-7)

God was willing to look at his creation, his beloved children, with candor. His willingness to look with candor resulted in an intellectual, emotional, and behavioral response. Intellectually, God accurately assessed the condition of humankind. He didn't make excuses for them nor did he take responsibility for the way they chose to live their lives and relate to him. Because God's heart and mind does not need clarifying, he trusted his perception and his understanding. Emotionally, the rejection of his love by his children caused great pain in his heart. It's hard for us to understand how the eternal God experiences pain in his heart, but Scripture is clear in saying that mankind's offenses against God were costly to his heart, so much so that he was grieved that he created humans. Behaviorally, God took definitive action to destroy the ones who had so violated relationship with him. He brought a flood that destroyed all life on earth except those saved through Noah and the ark.

Clearly God was not feeling sorry for himself, blaming others for his behaviors, whining, or having a pity party. The offenses against God were significant and deeply disturbing and required a devastating response. Notice that God did not just patiently and quietly "love" people until they realized their errors and came back to him. Decisions were made and action was taken without their ever "getting it."

So when a spouse violates his or her mate in marriage, the wrongdoing must be understood as a disturbing offense that causes wounds in the heart and requires some sort of action. God takes violations very seriously and so should we. The point of this chapter is not to discuss what to do with the offenses but to acknowledge that offenses cause wounds resulting in meaningful suffering. Only when the disturbance is appropriately understood and wounds are acknowledged can the heart respond with wisdom and strength. If it is not recognized, relational sin will continue to destroy a marriage.

We are taking time in this chapter to strongly acknowledge a reality that is rarely taken seriously in the Christian community. *The reality is that many people suffer greatly in difficult marriages.* We are often so focused on getting help for marriage or simply "turning it over to Christ" that we miss the agony of a heart groaning over shattered dreams or evil assaults on its soul. It is in your agony that you will sense the spiritual war for your soul that is expressed through "groaning." Thankfully, there is great hope for those who suffer wisely.

Let us give you a note for wisdom. When suffering, you need both strength to endure and a plan for how to get through the pain and confusion of a wounded heart. Many well-intentioned people will offer only a *strategy* when what you really need is the *strength* to know that God is still in this with you and will give you the courage to continue. Sometimes people don't need truths thrown at them; they need someone to journey with them, someone who knows, who understands, who gives strength to continue on. Instead of listening to the pressure of those who tell you what to do to get beyond your pain, surround yourself with people who understand the hellish torment of the journey. Find others who will lend you their strength and will not pummel you with what you "ought" to do. If someone's marriage is without significant pain and struggle, thinking about difficulties in marriage is more an academic exercise for them than a soul-gripping passion. Like Job's counselors, their "biblically correct" advice will sound logical and well-intentioned but will have little to do with the realities you are experiencing in your heart. Find friends who will engage in the battle for your heart.

Understanding Wounds: Neglect, Abandonment, Assault

You'll best understand wounds as you continue to clarify the desires and agendas of your heart. In order to know what is wrong, you must first know what is right. Beneath the pain of each wound is a desire.

The desire may come from a good heart or a bad heart. Our intention is to help you identify the desires beneath the wounds and explore them until you can embrace the dignity within you, repent of any corruption, and live from your God-given desires. This will not eliminate suffering but will allow a suffering that leads to life instead of death. When the path to life is seen, thriving will be possible.

Neglect — The Experience of Being Orphaned

Definition: Neglect is the lack of positive engagement in your life resulting in loneliness and poverty of heart. You feel as if you are invisible. Your heart is deprived of nourishment because what you hunger and thirst for has never been given to you.

If God has designed you with chambers in your heart that long for intimacy, mutual purpose, and absolute trust, your spouse's neglecting your heart will result in wounds. The pain is felt to the degree you become alive to your desires. Rather than having the experience of being completed, enjoyed, and enhanced by your spouse, you are aware of an emptiness that results in intense loneliness. The chambers of your soul groan with desire.

Throughout history a debate has raged as to whether it is better to have never been loved or to have been loved and lost that love. Since the chambers of your heart are designed to thrive when they are full, both situations cause significant wounds. To never have been loved means your heart will never experience the nourishment necessary to become strong and powerful. Most professionals in the counseling field believe the wounds of neglect are as damaging as the most severe emotional wounds, including grief experienced with the death of a loved one, and the pain of abuse.

Orphan — Never Loved

The orphan is present and his basic needs are attended to, but no attempt is made to connect with him. The orphan is living with someone who is his one-flesh partner but who functions as a cold, disinterested caretaker. What was thought to be caring was caretaking. What was believed to be enjoying was exploiting. The wounds of an orphan occur over time. The orphan comes to realize his spouse has never cherished him or ever wanted to know who he is. He has never known or been known as a "beloved." In his marriage he is, has been, and will always be alone.

Patrick and Adriana

Adriana could no longer deny the pain in her heart. For over twenty years she had believed that Patrick truly loved her but was so busy providing for the family he just couldn't get more involved with her. Everything he did was for good reasons — for the kids, the church, or his work. Though her heart suffered from neglect, she had always believed the time would come when they would rest from all their busyness and devote their energies to each other. She clung to the hope that Patrick really wanted intimacy with her as badly as she wanted it with him. The nest would be empty, career ambitions would be fulfilled, and all obstacles inhibiting closeness would be eliminated.

When their youngest went away to college, Adriana's dreams for this new season were not meaningful to Patrick. Instead of seeking deeper connection with her, he found new mountains to climb. The truth that he really did not ask her to complete him was becoming more apparent. It began exposing a wound she had never acknowledged. She knew her husband didn't show interest in exploring and enhancing the feminine heart within her, a heart that was now crying out with plaintive sounds that left her unsettled. The realization that she could never get back the lost years, the ones she had lovingly and sacrificially offered him, devastated her and made her feel so foolish for ignoring the warnings her gut had repeatedly sounded. She had trusted in the ideal of a one-flesh marriage that Patrick had no intention of fulfilling. Shame and self-hatred beat down any sense of respect she had left. Why had she believed him? Was she so weak and needy that she didn't have the courage to see that she didn't matter to him?

What about the future? Could she pick up the pieces? Her whole life had been focused by the hope that she and Patrick would have their day when they would truly be one in flesh, spirit, and purpose. Who had she been to him all those years? Why did she allow him to neglect the things that were most important to her? The stunning realization that he really did not care drained life from her spirit with merciless mocking. He said he cared and would do anything for her, but she knew he did not have any idea what her heart longed for and had no interest in finding out. His disdain and impatience was felt every time she attempted to share with him the concerns and longings of her heart. Lying next to him after another empty sexual encounter, she gazed toward the darkened ceiling in her bedroom, sensed the contentment in her husband's sleep, and realized no one would ever know the grief of her silent night. She was alone, knowing her journey of suffering would not be shared or healed by another.

Some have described the ache of loneliness in marriage as more painful than death. At least the death of a spouse is final and explainable. The body is a lifeless corpse that cannot offer love or rejection. While a spouse may rage against that reality, the logic of it cannot be denied and, to some degree, provides an acceptable explanation for loneliness. But the utter rejection by a person who has the capacity to offer love defies logic and does not offer a satisfying reason for the neglect of a willing heart. *"Why? What have I done? What is it about me that is so unacceptable? How do I fix this? I can't stop being me!"*

Adriana's realization brought home the reality that she had lived in her marriage as an *orphan* who was never loved. The vibrant chambers in her heart had never experienced the joy of her husband's warm passion. Every day Adriana suffered with the agonizing awareness that her soul was designed to be entered by the man sitting across from her at the breakfast table, and it would never happen. A child who is orphaned is separated from the life-giving and life-enhancing energies of a parent's love and care. Without this stimulating love, the chambers of a child's heart are never entered and are unable to grow and strengthen. He or she is left to cry out in emptiness and despair. The unnurtured chambers of the orphan's heart put the child at great risk for all sorts of developmental delays and even premature death.

This emptiness is what Christ experienced when he encountered the rejection, the neglect of the life and love he longed to share with his beloved.

> O Jerusalem, Jerusalem, the city that kills the prophets and stones those who are sent to it! How often would I have gathered your children together as a hen gathers her brood under her wings, and you would not! (Matthew 23:37)

Once again God expressed his deep desire to be embraced by his people. God knows relational neglect and feels the pain of rejected love. In this verse, Christ also indicates how much he longed to enhance the lives of his children by sending them prophets and offering his wise protection. A wounded heart may be neglected not only by what is not given it but also by the unwillingness of the beloved to receive its strength and beauty.

Abandonment — The Experience of Being Widowed

> *Definition: Abandonment is the removal of positive engagement in your life resulting in shame and despair of heart. You are forsaken and feel exposed as being defective and undesirable. Your heart is raw and empty because that which you once received and gave has been taken from you.*

In chapter 4, we discussed the devastation rejection brings upon a heart. Whereas the orphan has the experience of longing for a love that has never been, the widow has the pain of experiencing the ongoing loss of what she had once known but will never know again. Rather than feeling complete as she did when she would give of herself and respond to her beloved, she now lives with a punishing awareness of loss.

We also described the devastating pain a rejecting spouse inflicts. Part of the torture of abandonment is that the widower cannot escape the humiliation of being deemed unacceptable or defective. He is left confused and fears that since his wife knew him, something bad about him must have caused her to leave him. Since everyone wrestles with feeling unacceptable or inadequate, abandonment triggers powerful insecurities. The wounds are ripped open each time the widow's husband gives his attention and heart energies elsewhere. To sit at home, abandoned and with intense loneliness, and to know that your spouse is feeling alive elsewhere is agonizing. *"Something bad about me is causing you to give your heart somewhere else."* It's a lie, of course, but it is experienced as truth.

In addition to causing the shame of being rejected, abandonment also produces the crushing pain of betrayal. *"I trusted the vow! I believed your good heart! I feel so humiliated and foolish for believing in you. What an idiot I am for having been so naïve as to have trusted my heart with you!"* And then the rage begins. *"What kind of person are you, anyway? Do you just give up, huh? You don't have the guts to face me? Or are you so shallow that all our years together mean nothing to you? You'd rather go play!"* But the rage is toothless and hides impotency. Despite all the groanings and expressions of anger, the widow or widower has no power to make the marriage come back to life. His or her spouse is dead though still breathing. There is no way to access him or her. Tears or rage are meaningless and powerless.

Widow — Loved and Forsaken

> *It's like taking your clothes off in front of your spouse only to see a look of disapproval or disgust in his or her eyes. "I have seen*

*you, I have known you, and now I no longer want you. I reject
you! Go away. You no longer interest me. I have fallen out of
love with you." — Chapter 4*

The widow has the experience of having celebrated one-flesh connection with her husband but has been abandoned and forced to exist in a
state of irretrievable loss of what was and what might have been.

Being aware that you've been widowed while your spouse is still
alive inflicts a torturous paradox within the heart. The torture a widow
or widower feels becomes extreme at the times when their spouse *does*
desire to connect, such as on a vacation or during a family celebration.
A taste of life and closeness is experienced but lost when the party is
over and once again they are abandoned. The wound is reopened, causing more pain and confusion.

Rich and Liz

Rich lived life at a steady pace. When they married, Liz was twenty-one,
seven years younger than him. What she appreciated most about Rich
was the stability he brought to her chaotic life. He was a solid, caring
man with a good heart who was true to his word. When their youngest
child started first grade, Rich agreed to work some overtime and also to
give up working out in order to watch the kids so that it would be possible for Liz to spend the three years needed to finish her college degree.

As she spent more time with the new people she met in school, he
confessed his concern that he was beginning to feel less a part of her
life and more like a roommate than a husband. They had always been
able to talk about anything, so he wasn't ready for her sharp retort. She
responded with a biting criticism of his controlling ways and of his lack
of ambition and desire for personal growth. "Stop being so insecure and
get a life like I finally did!" was what she told him in response to his pleas.
Rich was dumbfounded and confused. He never suspected she was discontent with their life together. They had been so close and so happy. He
told her he did have a life, one that was happily united with hers.

Liz lost weight, tanned, and spent more and more time away from him, often not coming home until the early morning hours. The ache in Rich's heart hammered away like the pain of a fifty-pound anvil being repeatedly dropped on his chest. He knew he wasn't as sharp as her professors and the guys she talked to in school. Rich couldn't compete with the sort of excitement she had found outside the home either. What he could offer her once meant so much but now seemed of little value to her. He had believed in her and was as loyal as a man could be to a wife. Devotion to his children's academic and spiritual education flowed powerfully from his heart's deep chamber for purpose. While going camping with the kids on weekends may not have thrilled Liz as much as discussions energized by current ideas and strong intellect and expressed through the disinhibiting effects of alcohol, Rich had hoped she could still enjoy their times of togetherness and value his sincere desires to share his life with her.

White-water rafting, exploring new trails, and exhausting themselves by mountain biking with the kids appeared to no longer hold interest for her. Actually, Liz had lost her desire for anything Rich had to offer. She told him it was time to grow up. He knew it was only a matter of months or even weeks before she no longer would require the security his paycheck provided. The loneliness of an abandoned widower was his closest companion. He no longer made a difference in her life. He had no weight or influence and had lost the one who had once delighted in his strengths.

Assault — The Experience of Being Hunted

> *Definition: Assault is invasive and destructive engagement in your heart resulting in feelings of violation and turmoil. You are frightened and feel as if you are disfigured. Your heart is twisted and torn because something has been crushed within you.*

When a person is neglected or abandoned, he is left on his own to make sense of what has happened. His spouse has removed herself and left him alone to try to figure out why he is deemed to be unworthy of love. This is not the case with assault. Spouses who assault their mates do so accompanied by messages of how they see their mates. The assault is always intended to accomplish a selfish agenda. The attacker either ignores the cries of the spouse or feels justified for inflicting wounds.

The Hunted—Loss of Self

The person who is hunted poses a threat to his or her spouse. His or her spouse will attempt to destroy or neutralize anything in the hunted mate that cannot be controlled. This may be accomplished with a warm smile or a menacing glare. The hunted not only suffers the wound of a loss of trust in his or her own instincts but also can lose a complete sense of his or her own identity.

Almost all of what a dangerous spouse (see chapter 6) does is assaultive. But don't think assaults always come in the form of emotional aggression and hostility. One of the best examples of the wounds from assault is an old black-and-white movie *Gaslight*. It is a simple story, yet right on target. A charming man searches out a young woman who could provide him access to a fortune in jewels, a fact of which she is ignorant. He wins her confidence, gets her absolute trust, and marries her. Then he uses her belief in him to break down her confidence in her ability to rely on her own judgment and perception of reality. She becomes entirely dependent on him to make sense of her increasingly bizarre life. Of course, he never discloses that once she serves her purpose of providing him access to the place where the jewels are hidden, his real agenda is to have her declared insane so he can get her out of the way. Her emotions, perceptions, intellect, and loyalties were attacked and wounded by a man who appeared to be devoted to her well-being.

Attacks from those who use biting sarcasm disguised as humor may not be unmasked and seen as attacks until the attackers have crossed a line and exposed their mean spirit. Assaults from overtly nasty people are painful but usually easy to recognize. These ragers, punishers, and demeaning spouses are not typically trying to change you. What they want is for you to suffer for any real or potential pain you may cause them. You are most likely a threat because of your gender. That's why the attack usually targets something about how you function as a male or a female. By attacking you they not only punish you and eliminate you as a threat, but they feel a sense of power and control. The more you fear them the more satisfied and safe they feel.

Attacks from a spouse who professes to want to help you are disarming and may take years to recognize. Many of the "nice" spouses who assault are consumers and exploiters who have convinced themselves they really are trying to help their mate become a better person—and sometimes they are, which makes matters more confusing. Because you want to believe your spouse is "for" you, you are likely to absorb many blows before you begin to listen to the pain from your wounds. A shrewd attacker neutralizes not only their spouse but also any resources that could be helpful to provide support and perspective. Friends are criticized, involvement with family is discouraged, and the church is charmed into believing he or she is a wonderful, caring servant. No one is allowed to see the hunter in action.

The attacker is usually brilliant at masking his or her true agenda. One way of attacking is by getting the spouse to debate the merits of what is being said in the attack and miss the fact the or she is being assaulted. Don't be trapped into wondering if your spouse is right or wrong when an attack is occurring. The assaultive spouse is able to use truth or deception in order to diminish the value and worth of her spouse. It is the *agenda* that is the key point. The agenda is to inflict harm.

The spouse who assaults with disparaging words attempts to wound the heart with shame, humiliation, and powerlessness. The belittling statement always has enough truth in it to disarm any counterattack. A masterful assault will resurrect childhood wounds of devastation and leave a spouse shattered. The cumulative effect of such assaults is that the wounded spouse despairs of wanting anything good and battles despair of life in his or her heart.

The hunted spouses experience both wounds and losses. They are wounded in their identity, their emotions, and their ability to trust their own perspectives. Losses include the loss of trust in the goodness of their spouse's heart, the loss of hope for a mutually satisfying marriage, and the loss of safety. The most significant loss, though, is the loss of self.

A person who has been hunted by his spouse is never loved and appreciated for who he is. His "self" must be eliminated, punished, or changed into a more acceptable form. The ability to express self and have a voice within the marriage is lost. As a result, he is wounded in his emotions. These people fear upsetting their husbands or wives by doing something that could trigger an assault and often develop anxiety resulting in panic attacks. They may be so used to being beat up they get away from the pain by numbing themselves into a depression. The wounded spouses may try to avoid attacks by mindlessly trying to eliminate whatever displeases their mates and desperately try to please them.

The tragedy is that by the time a hunted spouse realizes how he has been damaged by the attacks, he feels he has lost himself and has nothing left. Many men believe they are losers who are unable to make a meaningful difference anywhere, especially in their wife's life. They believe they are defective as men. Women accept that they have nothing any healthy person would desire. Their beaten and battered spirits leads them to think they are unacceptable and repulsive. Resigning themselves to a hopeless life of pain or getting far away from their spouse may appear like the only possible ways to survive.

FACING WOUNDS

The wounds experienced in a difficult marriage do not heal easily, if ever. Neglect, abandonment, and assault cause the heart to suffer. Suffering is most severe when you have no means of protecting your heart from the ongoing offenses against it. The orphan and widow have experienced the demise of their marriage and face the painful prospect of having to grieve the merciless power of death on a daily basis. Their life will include ongoing mourning. The assaulted heart encounters evil like that found in a sadistic terrorist whose sick passion is to revel in causing misery and ripping open scarring wounds. The wounded heart struggles to survive as the Enemy urges yielding to despair, bitterness, or self-loathing. It may feel masochistic to keep a wounded heart alive in the face of ongoing neglect, abandonment, or assault. Why stand up again just to be knocked down?

Suffering has been part of humankind's lot since Creation, and the issue of how to understand and face suffering has been addressed by many of the best minds, past and present, who have written and spoken on the human condition. Since Jesus suffered on the cross beyond any human suffering, his book is filled with guidance about how to embrace suffering with the hope in his restorative goodness. We believe that at some point every person will have to develop an understanding of how to face suffering, if he or she has not done so already. Certainly any Christian trying to reconcile an all-powerful, loving God with the horrendous suffering found among so many in this world must develop a way to understand and face suffering.

While we urge you to deeply engage in the lifelong search for how to journey with God through the suffering you face, for our purposes we are going to offer a specific direction that we believe will help you coexist with a wounded heart while thriving. *Remember, it is the heart that is most seriously attacked in a difficult marriage. Your goal is to learn how to keep your heart alive and thriving in the face of ongoing marital suffering.* Before we do so, we want you to take a look at some ways you may have chosen to manage the pain of wounds you have felt in your difficult marriage. In the next chapter we will explore four ways the wounded heart attempts to survive. Each path will feel like a legitimate way of surviving the pain of a wounded heart, but none of them leads to life or thriving. We urge you to prayerfully explore how you have dealt with the pain in your marriage and open yourself to a better way.

A SPECIAL WARNING ABOUT PHYSICAL ASSAULT

Physical assault needs to be in a category of its own. Many who are being emotionally assaulted or abused, both male and female, have told us they wish their spouse would physically assault them. They feel like the wounds from emotional assaults are deeper than most physical wounds, but no one can see them. If they were visible, the assaults could be more honestly confronted because the wound could not be denied by the assaulting spouse or anyone else.

Even though the human heart has limits to what it can endure, hope exists telling a spouse that good days will follow the dark ones. This is not always true with physical assaults. People die or they are permanently disfigured or impaired. While we believe the most difficult spouse cannot destroy a heart, we know he or she can destroy a body. If you are being physically abused or threatened, get help. Though many communities and even churches deny the reality of domestic violence, many others will reach out and help you. No one should have to suffer the torment of having to live with a physically abusive spouse. Your spouse is not likely to stop the threat of abuse until he or she has to answer to someone other than you.

CHAPTER 8

The Surviving Heart

*You have difficulty keeping your heart alive and
"good" in the face of ongoing disappointment.*

*Do not let my heart incline to any evil, to busy myself with
wicked deeds in company with men who work iniquity,
and let me not eat of their delicacies!*
— Psalm 141:4

Something has happened to your heart. The assaults on your heart have either made you stronger and moved you in good directions, or your good heart is being corrupted and moving you in bad directions. What does the orphan do when she realizes her husband is never going to offer her a meaningful relationship where she can offer her heart and receive his loving care? How does the widower keep his heart strong and vibrant when his wife's disdain for him mocks his attempts to be a meaningful part of her life? And how can you offer good parts of your life to someone who is bent on tearing you down or using you with no regard for what is important to you?

You may be thinking, *Why do you think I'm reading this book? I wish I knew what to do, but I'm just trying to survive the storms!* That's it. Do you see it? You already have a strategy in place that's designed to get you through your difficulties. So before we talk about how you can thrive when your heart is wounded, you must first discover the tactics you've already put in place. When your heart is in survival mode, you are committed to moving in directions that are taking you away from a good heart and corrupting your desires. You are losing the battle. We need to take a good look at your surviving heart so you can change direction.

Let's think of four possible ways you have responded to what has been done to you. Each of these ways is a path that indicates you are moving in bad directions. Without thinking much about it, you've employed strategies you hope will best manage the pain of your wounded heart. The first strategy is to not resist but rather to accept whatever your spouse is offering you and give what's being asked of you. When you have been denied what your heart longs for, you can resign yourself to believing "this is as good as it's going to get" or "I just don't want to be hurt anymore." You can "give in" to your spouse and your despair and make the best of it.

The second thing you can do is say, "I need this like I need a hole in the head. I'm out of here!" and "get away." You can stay in your marriage and look like a really good spouse, but your heart is far from your marriage and your spouse. You've distracted yourself and have gone on to something else, someone else, or some other activity that has consumed your heart. You may do that in an overt way where everyone can see it, or you may do it in a covert way where no one sees it. But you are gone! You're not going to get hurt again. Nobody's going to mess with you anymore. You'll never ask for anything so no one will get the chance to neglect you. You're done, and you get away from the pain, the heart-wrenching barbs your spouse throws your way.

The third way of surviving the wounds inflicted by your spouse is to "get even." You decide to stay in the marriage, but you're going to spend your life making your spouse pay for all the junk he or she has done to you. *"I'll stay, but you'll pay!"* The chambers of your good heart that are designed for purpose and integrity are so corrupted that you believe the best way to satisfy them is to get revenge. So your whole being becomes dedicated to letting your spouse know how much you loathe him, how much he disgusts you, how badly he's hurt you, and that you will never, ever, *ever* give him a chance to hurt you again. You will punish her for everything she's ever done to you. You will despise her, and humiliate her. And you may do it in subtle ways or in overt ways.

You are the victim. Of course, once you take the position that you are the defined victim, you can never be blamed for anything again. You are always right, you are always entitled to your pain, and your spouse is never entitled to his or her pain. You define the relationship: "I've been hurt, you are my offender, and, no matter what you do, that's the way it's going to be."

The fourth coping strategy is similar to the third one but has some key differences. You say that you are wounded and your spouse is to blame, and you choose to be an open wound the rest of your life. *"I am suffering, I have been hurt so badly, and you wouldn't dare hurt me again, would you?"* You will constantly "get attention" because you are so wounded. *"Don't ask anything of me. Please don't hurt me again."* You will constantly monitor your spouse to see if the spouse will give you affection, to see if he or she really loves you, and to see if he or she is doing anything that could hurt you.

A great example is what often occurs when a husband has been caught viewing pornography. Of course, pornography is cancerous to a marriage and has no place in a godly life or healthy marriage, but a wounded spouse getting attention protects herself by micromanaging her offending husband's life. *"What were you looking at? Why were you looking at her? I know what you were thinking. Why do you continue to hurt me when you know how hard it is for me? I have the right to monitor every movement you make so that you never, ever, ever hurt me again!"*

As we go through these four ways of surviving a difficult spouse and a difficult marriage, please, please don't try to find your spouse in this. That will be your tendency because you're human. Make sure you come back to *you* and ask God to help *you* find yourself and the ways you have not loved well when you've been disappointed. Remember what the problem is: *You have difficulty keeping your heart alive and good in the face of ongoing disappointment.* You're not going to thrive if your focus is on your spouse. It's just not going to happen. We often tell strugglers we wish we could put a little microchip into their brain that would get them to not focus on what has been done to them but rather on what has happened inside them and how they have coped. So much time and pain could be saved if this were available. But it's not, so you will have to be convinced before you are willing to move past your wounds and embrace the battle for your heart.

The survival strategy you are using may have made sense at one point in your life. You may have developed it to cope with rejection from your father or hostility from your mother. It may have been the only way you could get through a tough childhood or other times of wounding. Once it was constructive and kept you going, but now it's doing you in. God has given you a good heart with stronger resources than you are using. But you won't move in a good direction from a good heart until you become aware of the bad direction you have taken.

What we want you to do is catch your (not your spouse's) behavior in one of these four ways of surviving. *"Oh yeah, I can see where I do that! Why do I do that? Well, I guess I do that because that's one of the ways I manage my pain or the difficulties in my marriage. But is it what I really want to be doing? Is it good?"* That's the question that you must focus on. Is this who you want to be? Is this direction coming from a good heart? This is where thriving begins to occur: when you look at what you're doing and you start to say, *"I don't want to be that person. I can't believe I've turned into this. Not only has my marriage been difficult, but look who I am! I'm a dead man who is caught up in busyness and addictions. I am a vengeful, angry, bitter person. I'm a whiner, and all I do is say how tough my life has been over and over again."*

When you catch yourself focusing on your spouse, stop and focus on your heart: *"God, I don't want to be this person, I don't want to show my kids this person. I can't go to sleep at night and say God's at peace and happy with my marriage. I can't do that. So I do not want to be this person—period! So Lord, help me to change. Help me to take the focus off my spouse."* But before you can do that, you need to take an in-depth look at the direction you have taken.

First, let's talk about pain again because we're going to talk about the role it plays in thriving in the following chapters. Every person reading this book and everyone we counsel wants to hear, "And when you figure this all out, the pain goes away." We wish that were the case. We wish this were a book that says to follow these principles and the pain will be gone. But we cannot in good conscience tell you that "thriving" means you have a lack of suffering, that when you change your ways your spouse will be thrilled and turn back to you, offering all your heart longs for. We are saying it in as many ways as we can because difficult marriages have ongoing suffering. If you have been orphaned or widowed and you have no access back, and your spouse continually refuses to engage in a healthy, godly relationship, you are going to be in pain. That is just the way it is. But identifying the strategies of your surviving heart is key. It is important to continue to clarify what it is that you want, to know what God wants for you, and to continue on in the cleansing process. This will free you from the confusion around your pain and from the shame/blame game—but it won't stop your pain. *Moving past your survival strategies will free you to begin to reclaim your life.* When you realize that life is difficult and you accept that all your dreams won't come true, you can focus on being determined to live and love for the sake of God, for those around you, and for your own well-being.

So let's get into the four survival strategies. A key characteristic shared by all four strategies is that they offer no way back. What we mean is that the goal of each strategy is survival. None of them gets into the problems of the heart in a way that provides hope for either reconciliation or thriving.

As you read these strategies, you will see they are describing things in an either/or way. *Either* you are living from your good heart *or* you are living from your bad heart. This is to emphasize the differences between two types of motivation. In reality, of course, you have only one heart that has mixed motives in every direction it takes.

GIVING IN

A person who gives in says, "I'm not going to fight this. I'm not going to fight your desire to control me, to punish me, to put me into a role that works for you and doesn't really consider me. I am just going to play that role to avoid conflict that I cannot resolve, primarily because I have no power to make things different. At least I get something from you, and something is better than nothing."

Another reason you may give in is because you have such a deep sense of failure and shame, inadequacy and unacceptability, that your spouse's mistreatment of you, to a large degree, makes sense. You give up on offering what you once desired to give because you now believe you have nothing valuable to offer. And so you deaden your desires, all the chambers of your soul have their lights turned off, and you dutifully go through life sometimes appearing to be happy, sometimes appearing to be nice. You take very few risks and learn not to ask much for yourself or offer much to your spouse.

We have a real problem with this in the Christian community. What we've just described can be dressed up and made to look like a wonderful husband and an amazing wife. Such a couple looks like model Christians because they don't have conflict; they don't argue, they are very submissive and gracious to each other, and they are, on one level, happy and content. But on another level, there ain't nobody home. God forbid if any real disturbance would occur in their marriage to disrupt the delicate fragility of the person who gives in. The person who gives in often says, "Don't get angry at me. Please don't be disappointed in me. Please don't tell me that I'm doing it wrong. Just tell me that I'm okay and that you still want to be with me." The victim can even convince himself or herself that it's not so bad after all. Or the person who gives in may "get it." He or she may think, *This is as good as it's going to be. I know I'm not being loved, sex is horrible, I don't really like my spouse, but as a noble martyr, I've gotta do what I've gotta* do. Yes, sometimes I wish he was dead, I wish sometimes that I had married somebody else or weren't married at all, but what good does it do to think about things like that? This is my lot in life, and I'll make the best of it for the kids, for God, for whatever.

Now what's wrong with that? Maybe that sounds like thriving, going forward despite. What's wrong with it is that it is not a self-, spouse-, or God-honoring relationship. If you learn not to ask anything from your spouse out of fear, you are agreeing to let your wife or husband set a bad direction from his or her corrupted heart. If you learn to accept whatever crumbs are thrown your way because you can't bear conflict or rejection, you may be encouraging your spouse to sin. You also will be modeling weakness for your children and causing them to continue the pattern you've started (or continued from one of your parents). Many people who are married to a destructive spouse—an alcoholic, an intimidator, or a passive, irresponsible person—never resist, never fight back, never challenge. If you challenge, there may be too big a price to pay, or it's too much work. So you give up: That's it; my life is over.

THE FOUR SURVIVAL STRATEGIES

Survival Strategy	Relational Energy	Heart Condition	Blind To:	Heart Noise
Give In	Yield	Numb	Despair	Muted
Get Away	Escape	Apathetic	Deception	Silent
Get Even	Attack	Bitter	Self-righteousness	Roaring
Get Attention	Consume	Fearful	Desperation	Moaning

Some people acknowledge they are giving up, and some people deny it. The sad thing is that many people are empty souls who are just existing, and they have no clue. No conflict, a little mistreatment, and life is good. But it isn't: God didn't call you to be dead but to thrive. If you have given in, you have lost the battle for your heart. Rather than expressing the strength and beauty God has placed within your heart, the chambers of your heart are silent except for muffled groans no one hears. If you give in, you agree to *neglect*—both your and your spouse's heart.

Getting Away

Faced with irresolvable dilemmas in your marriage, you believe you have nothing to offer that will make a difference. There is no way to change your situation, or perhaps you've figured it's too much work. You don't want to just give in because you can't bear the pain, so you manage your wounded heart and avoid pain by getting away from the assaults and rejection. There are many ways to get away from the difficulties and pain in your marriage. You can get away physically, mentally, and emotionally.

One objective of getting away is never having to offer what you don't want to give or get what you don't want to receive, minimizing the chance to experience pain. One more is finding a way to numb the pain your wounded heart feels. You find something, anything, to deaden the pain and help you not think about your painful marriage. A great danger in this strategy is separating so far away that you develop your own world containing only you and your thoughts. No one in, no one out.

Another objective of getting away is finding a way to satisfy your desires while minimizing risk of rejection or failure. A prime example is a man escaping by using pornography. Why does a wounded man go to pornography? Because he finds no conflict there, no woman needing something from him that he can't or doesn't want to give, like patience. He won't have the hassles being with his wife would bring. He has no weight of responsibility; therefore he has no pain, no risk of failure or shame. More important, for the rejected or assaulted husband, he has found a place where, for a brief time, he can feel powerful, alive, and wanted by someone who will not hurt him. The problem is that he has chosen a wrong direction, one that can never satisfy the thirsts of his good heart or fulfill his desire for a God-honoring, one-flesh relationship.

There is a time to disengage from the destructive aspects of a marriage and get away. Limiting a destructive spouse access to your heart is wisdom. The difference between protecting your heart out of wisdom and using a survival strategy is the difference between thriving and surviving, which we will discuss in depth in the next chapter. A person with a thriving heart has embraced disappointment, fought off corruption, and finds joy in the healthy desires in the chambers of his or her heart. Thrivers strive to communicate to their spouse that they are available for healthy, godly relationship, and refuse to engage in destructive involvement. The directions they take are motivated by a good heart and are healthy and godly.

The surviving heart that gets away is reactive and doesn't think through the problems we have outlined in this book. Survivors avoid the issues and settle with managing their pain by distracting themselves, giving up on their marriage, or gratifying their desires in superficial or destructive ways. "Getting away" is disengagement without resolving the issues of the heart. A surviving person doesn't access the best energies of a good heart. A thriving heart goes through the issues, as opposed to going around them or avoiding them.

A woman may keep busy with all sorts of activities to distract herself and numb her pain rather than offer herself from her good heart. What may appear to be a good direction, involvement with kids or ministry, driven by a good heart is actually a good direction motivated by a weak, frightened heart. *"I'm busy with the kids, with my parents, or with the ladies' Bible study in order to avoid you. I fill every moment of my day so I can't be available to anyone who could hurt me, disappoint me, and ask things I don't want to give."*

People who get away are often "done" with their spouses. Their desire for their mate has died, and it feels like it can never be revived. They have died to their marriage but have not reclaimed the healthy thirsts within their heart and set off in good directions. Is this you? Are you the person we have described who has read all the books and done all the praying, but your spouse hasn't budged? You have come to realize that he or she is not interested in change. While you may be right, as we agree with you that some spouses are not likely to change, you may now see that your survival strategy has been to get away, to remove access to your mind, body, and emotions in a way that doesn't lead to life. Surviving in a difficult marriage by continually numbing your pain or by finding heart satisfaction in wrong directions causes you to lose the battle for your heart. The spouse who gets away agrees to abandon her husband's heart and relieve her heart with an illegitimate substitute.

GETTING EVEN

This is the way of surviving that feeds the darkest instinct of the corrupt heart: revenge. *"I will stay, but you will pay! I will never let you have peace because of all that you have done to me. Direct and indirect messages of how angry I am at you and how I despise you will follow you like a swarm of raging bees. After the price I have paid for putting up with you, don't even think of criticizing me. Let's get this straight—I'm right and you are wrong. Any pain you get from me you've got coming to you. And don't ever believe you can do anything that would make up for what you've done. But you had better keep trying to atone because I'll make you pay if you don't!"*

One friend who read this description said it appeared to be a bit extreme. He thought no one with a wounded heart sees himself or herself as *all* right and the spouse as *all* wrong. We're not sure we agree.

After I (Mike) introduced the "get even" survival strategy at a staff meeting, one of the women on our staff said, "Mike, you're going to have a real problem with this book." When I asked why, she said, "Because most of the women who are reading this book, who are in a difficult marriage, will say they already know what they want, they know what they desire, and they know all about the pain in their marriage. They will say they know about their own responsibility, what they have done, and what it is like to live with them. But they have locked in on their husband, and he is the problem. And until he 'gets it,' they will not budge. They will take no responsibility for how they treat their husband and will feel fully justified when they attack him. I don't think these women will be able to look at themselves. This is why they are divorcing at alarming rates. They are done with 'the jerk' and can find no reason to stay and work things through when they have a chance to be happier without him."

I think she is right. I counsel many women who are "done" and will not stop shredding their husbands. But it's not hard to understand what gets them to the place where they become hardened toward their husband. In the beginning of a marriage, a woman tends to trust her husband, believing he has her best interests in mind. She is willing to overlook his selfishness, weakness, irresponsibility, and lack of regard for her. She thinks, *This guy must be okay. I mean, he's a decent guy. My parents thought he was okay, and the church likes him.* And so she denies the internal warning signs that something is wrong. She denies the internal voice that says, *You're not being treated well. He's not who he says he is.*

They deny and deny and deny until the time comes when they have had enough. There comes that point when the wife has an awakening. She realizes her husband is not going to change, he doesn't get it, and she will never be heard or intimately loved. A wife who has trusted that her husband has had a good heart toward her reacts violently to the sense of betrayal she feels when she begins to think she has been "played" by him. *"You have betrayed the good thing that I have given you. I have given you the best of myself, from a good heart, with a good agenda, and now I see you're a con man, a charmer, a selfish person who has everyone believing what a great guy you are. And I am done with you. I'm done! But I'm not just done* (remember our desire for integrity and justice); *I haven't had a whole lot of justice and fairness in my life."* Many spouses who struggle in their marriage bring a history of betrayal into their marriage and look to their spouse as their savior, unfortunately.

She then says, *"I am done with pain and with being blamed by you!"*

The dark side of her almost delights in causing her husband to twist and writhe while he protests, begs, or pleads. But there is no way in the world she is going to open up her heart and allow him in. And she can be as cold as she can be, and she can be as harsh as she can be, while having no twinge of regret. Counseling ends when the counselor says to her, "What do you think it's like for him when you [fill in the blank]?" She's done because she's made a deal with the counselor, her pastor, or her friends to never, ever focus on her part of the problem. Since she is managing the pain in her heart by assaulting her husband with his failures and making him pay, any attempt to expose her survival strategy is experienced as an attack, reopening her wound. So she's done. *"I'll stay, but you'll pay."*

Nothing good comes from this survival strategy. The tragedy is that they both pay. If he does take responsibility for the pain he has caused her, she will not allow him back into her heart. Her desire for vengeance is corrupted and moves in a wrong direction. Neither will know joy.

While we're using a wife as an example, wounded men are equally destructive when they get even with their wives for real or imaginary offenses. Men can intimidate, terrorize, and punish with a hostility tinged with covert threats of physical violence. Many wounded men combine the strategy of "getting away" with "getting even" by withdrawing and withholding. They grow silent but let their wives feel their hostility and contempt with their disdainful facial expressions, dark moods, and one-word, sarcastic dismissals.

If you see yourself in this category, pray that God will break you from the nearly intoxicating rush you feel when you blast away. You are better than this. You must reenter the battle for your heart's sake and keep it alive in healthy ways.

GETTING ATTENTION

The spouse who gets attention lives from an open wound, managing his hurts by calling his spouse to view him through his pain. The pain may have been caused by her, life, or God, but being a wounded person has become his identity. It is how he sees himself and how he wants others to see him, especially his wife. *"Please understand that I am a wounded, hurting person. If you are not careful, you could hurt me again. I'm not sure you understand this so I will continually let you know how difficult my life is. Don't ask too much of me because I have so little left to give."* He has not been able to give in and hide his wounds, numbing the chambers of his heart. Unable to mobilize his resources, perhaps because he can't bear the thought of being alone, he has not found a way to get away. His heart is not embittered to the point where he would strike back, and he may lack the assertiveness or the rage to try to get even. He fears that if he is too aggressive in blaming his spouse, she may leave him.

Women tend to be more on the surface as they get attention, while men sulk and play the martyr, expressing irritation when their wives don't understand all the pain they feel for being attacked and criticized. Often men don't verbally express how they feel but instead keep an active "woe is me" tragedy going on in their mind. *"She doesn't appreciate how much I sacrifice for the family and how little (sex) I get in return. I work my butt off for her, and it's never enough. I resent her for not letting me do things I want to do for me."* Men have creative ways of letting their wives know how pained they are. Often they are the "nice guys" who try so hard to please and just want to be loved and appreciated in return. When they don't get what they want, they are crushed.

A wife who gets attention often lives a life of drama, filled with crises centered on her fears of experiencing more pain. Her spouse is often both a hero and a villain. If only he would understand how badly he hurt her and give her assurances that he will love her and never hurt her again (hero), she would be free from her pain. But he can't guarantee he will never hurt her (villain), and so the wounded spouse lives a life of pain, continually being hurt and disappointed. She must constantly monitor everything he does or says to be sure he is not hiding anything that could hurt her. She is likely to view what he says and does through suspicious, accusatory eyes. Always misunderstood and unappreciated, she groans in despair and desire for the love she fears she will never know.

A different type of spouse who gets attention is the one who continually criticizes himself for messing up in his marriage. This shame-based person lets it all out by degrading himself and keeping the self-loathing wound wide open. His hope is that he will get the love he wants by being such a wretched creature of low esteem that his spouse will offer him reassurances (which he will never really believe) that he isn't as bad as he is saying and (often said with forced sincerity) that she really loves him and, again, is so sorry for the ways she has hurt him. If the wounded person can't manipulate this response, he may get more attention by becoming physically ill or clinically depressed.

Please don't think we are poking fun—we are not. Our hope is that if this describes you, you will see it as a survival strategy that has corrupted your good heart far more than the wounds inflicted by your spouse have. It is likely you have brought a history of woundedness into your marriage and need to discover where you developed your coping strategy. But if you are handling your wounds by getting attention, the Enemy is winning the battle for your heart. There is a better way.

In chapter 2, we said that one of the issues that needed to be clarified in understanding marital difficulties is knowing what you long to receive and then offering what is good. You can experience severe pain when you ask to have a corrupted desire met and are refused. As you examine the survival strategies that best describe you, pray for clarity. Ask that you will be able to discern and have confidence that the wounds you are surviving are caused by unmet desires that come from a good heart and not a bad heart. If you are not clear, seek the counsel of some wise people, especially those who know you well, to help you clarify the motives of your heart.

It is our hope that you will spend meaningful time and prayer trying to determine the directions you have taken in order to survive in your difficult marriage. Seek the wisdom and strength to focus not on your spouse but on your own response to what he or she has brought your way. If you can see that you may not have loved well from a good heart, then the ideas for thriving in the next chapters will be able to offer you hope.

PART 4

Transcending Suffering

THRIVING DESPITE

CHAPTER 9

Freedom and Disengagement

*And it is my prayer that your love may abound more and more, with
knowledge and all discernment, so that you may approve what is
excellent, and so be pure and blameless for the day of Christ.*

— *Philippians 1:9-10*

You are now getting ready to move further down the path toward the
thriving heart. But there's one more hurdle we're going to have to pass
through in order to firmly move in that direction. Great joy is ahead for
you, as well as peace and contentment. You can get up in the morning
and say, "I'm feeling good about life, about God, and I know I have a
future. I'm moving forward with purpose and integrity." You can say
this even if you are more aware than ever how difficult your marriage is
and even if you are still suffering. Remember that the path to freedom
and thriving runs through *you*, not your spouse. The hurdle you must
pass contains all the ways you defend against allowing your heart to be
transformed through brokenness.

AWARENESS — WHAT HAVE I BECOME?

One of the great heroes of literature is found in Victor Hugo's epic
novel, *Les Misérables.* Jean Valjean was a man who lived life fully and

passionately. He had a loving, good heart and offered his strengths for the well-being of those around him, even his enemies. But the journey to living from a good heart followed a difficult path as he had lived a painful life, one that caused him to lose the battle (but not the war!) for his heart. As a young man he faced a great moral dilemma. His family was starving because France was in a severe depression and he couldn't find work to earn money to buy food. In his desperation he decided to steal a single loaf of bread to feed them. He was caught, arrested, and sentenced to work as a slave in a brutal prison where men were treated as less than human. After nineteen years of imprisonment, Valjean emerged from that prison with a dark heart. A broken and bitter man, he was filled with hate and felt justified for lashing out against the world.

At that time in France when prisoners were released, they were treated as outcasts, dangerous men who were not allowed to work or live in towns. So when Valjean tried to reenter society, no one would associate with him except for a kindly old man, a bishop who welcomed him, fed him, and allowed him to stay in his modest home. But more than that, he saw that the chambers in Valjean's heart were dark and corrupted by hatred. The bishop dared to bring light to Valjean's bitter heart, even calling him his "brother." Valjean would not allow his heart to be entered by the light of the bishop's love and, instead, acted from his corrupt heart and moved in a dark direction, stealing the bishop's expensive silver. He was caught and brought back to the bishop so that he could be identified and returned to the hellish prison, where he would surely die.

The bishop was not motivated by a dark heart seeking vengeance and had Valjean released, saying the silver was a gift. He then handed him his silver candlesticks, scolding Valjean for "forgetting" them. This time the powerful light from the bishop's good heart pierced his wall of resistance, startling him. It reached into the chambers of his heart, turning on his own lights and causing great confusion in his soul. He was aware of something stirring in his heart in response to the powerful love the bishop offered. Rather than feeling the familiar, ugly darkness that had dominated his soul for so many years, Valjean became aware of a strong desire for what the bishop had—goodness.

Yet as light entered his soul, resonating with the good that had been covered over by bitterness, Valjean was stunned with an awareness of who he had become. The enormity of the corruptness of his soul shocked this man who had been brutalized by the worst mankind had to offer. But now he saw that he had become one of them, a man who lived from his selfish corruptness. He understood that the issue no longer concerned the evil that was done to him but how he had lost the battle for his heart. In the musical version of *Les Misérables*, Valjean is appalled when he sees he has become "a thief in the night, a dog on the run, and is the hour so late that nothing remains but the cry of my hate?"[1]

Valjean knew the dark, hateful man was not who he wanted to be. The bishop's willingness to enter his life showed him that God had a better way for him to live. He cried out, "Is there another way to go?" And he discovered the way of *life*, the way of *thriving*, the way that is available to you. You can become free of the darkness of your survival strategies. The pain of a difficult marriage no longer needs to define how you face the world. Life is available to you.

Are you ready? Let's just dip into this one more time, though we hope you will welcome this process as a way of life. Continue to pray that God will help you see the log in your own eye so that you can see clearly enough to remove the speck from your spouse's eye. A basic biblical principle is that it is through dying that we live and through brokenness that we are made whole.

BROKENNESS

Until you are broken, your human nature will cause you to stay consumed with the faults in your spouse, and you will not change. Brokenness will bring you to the end of yourself where you will cry, "God, teach this selfish heart how to move beyond self-interests and love in such a way that blesses and frees me from the darkness of trying to find my own justice!"

God doesn't say *don't* correct your brother, but that first your sin must appear as a log in your eye. Look at yourself first so that you may have the proper, unbiased perspective to accurately assess your brother. The idea is that you must allow and cultivate a healthy disturbance within you regarding your response to adversity. Your relational crud must disturb you as a log in your eye would. Only then can you have the sort of spiritual humility and power that will allow you to confront the speck or unrighteousness in your spouse. Until humility replaces pride, you cannot thrive.

Pride causes you to think that your sin and your offenses aren't nearly as severe as your spouse's. After all, you are reading books, going to counseling, and taking a good look at yourself. Humility calls you to say, "It's me, it's me, O Lord, standing in the need of prayer." What is stopping you from going there? Do you feel like you've been beat up enough and you're tired of feeling bad about yourself? Do you think your spouse will say that he or she is glad you've discovered that you've been the problem all along, letting him or her off the hook again? Remember that this is your journey. Let God help you see what has become of your heart and restore what was lost: the pure desires that come when his Spirit regains influence in your heart. Then you will regain the passion to thrive as God helps you win the battle for your heart.

So what will cause you to be broken? The same thing that broke Jean Valjean broke David and Peter: an exposure of the corruption in your heart. Review the strategies of the surviving heart on page 163. Which of those best describes you? The next time you catch yourself justifying a destructive survival strategy or find yourself being negative toward your spouse, think back to your best dreams about marriage. Did you want to become the sort of person who has such a dark attitude toward your mate (even if you think the behavior justifies your thoughts)? Say out loud, "I don't like what I see in my heart. There has got to be another way. Lord, help me restore my good heart."

It is not only awareness of the destructiveness of your survival strategies that will lead to brokenness. As humility displaces pride and self-righteousness in your heart, you will also become aware that a significant amount of your pain has been caused by corrupt desires. You have been unfair to your spouse, selfishly demanding unhealthy things and making him or her pay for not providing what you crave. You may discover that when you thought you were asking to be respected, you were really requiring your wife to never challenge you and make you feel insecure. You may realize that the anger you felt when your husband spent time with his college friends came from a heart that wanted to control and limit him and not, as you thought, from a heart that wanted to be loved by him.

Humility also opens the door to your own limitations. One reason a person remains stuck in a difficult marriage is because she thinks she ought to be able to find a way to get her spouse to change, and she won't stop until she does. This is pride. Humility allows a person to be broken of his belief that he can find the engineering to change his spouse. When a person is broken and at the end of himself, he will, in humility, be ready to yield to God and accept his limitations.

Our hope is that you are taking responsibility for who you are and for what you have done and that you are saying, "I don't want to be this person anymore. This is not who God made me to be. I'm not going to be negative, bitter, fearful, dead, angry, or whining." Moreover, "I'm not who I know I can become. I haven't taken what has happened to me and found the strength to respond with God's wisdom, and that's what I want." As this hits you, you may feel crushed and broken. You may shed tears even. (Yes, you may weep and have sleepless nights.) But this is a brokenness that leads to life, not to shame and debilitating guilt. True brokenness leads you to repentance, not self-hatred. Follow the prayer David prayed when Nathan exposed his dark heart following his selfish and destructive affair with Bathsheba: "Create in me a clean heart, O God, and renew a right spirit within me" (Psalm 51:10).

REPENTANCE

"All we like sheep have gone astray; we have turned — every one — to his own way; and the LORD has laid on him the iniquity of us all." (Isaiah 53:6)

"This confession is *unreserved*; there is not a word to detract from its force, nor a syllable by way of excuse. The confession is *a giving up of all pleas of self-righteousness*. It is the declaration of men who are consciously guilty — guilty with aggravations, guilty without excuse: they stand with their weapons of rebellion broken in pieces."[2]

Without understanding the corrupted desires that war with redeemed thirsts and without embracing the need for repentance, thriving in a difficult marriage will not be possible. Repentance, though extremely painful, is actually a positive, transforming experience and not a punishing one. Repentance and forgiveness allow you to be cleansed from the grime and mess that result from your marital battles. You long to feel clean and pure as you attempt to thrive while battling in the darkness of a difficult marriage. Repentance results in a clean heart and a restored hope.

Repentance requires you die to the destructive paths you are walking and begin to thirst for a better way. That's why it's important that you open yourself up to how other people see you, especially your spouse. Learn the ways you lessen who your spouse is by what you say, do, or think. Become aware of how you justify inner thoughts of disrespect, because you want to repent not only of dark directions in your treatment of her, but also of the dark inner attitudes you have cultivated in your heart. In order to be transformed and live from your thriving heart, you need to be open to ongoing brokenness and allow repentance to become a way of life.

A practical way to repent is to deal with the ways you manage your pain from your bad heart. When you are assaulted or neglected, you will be severely tempted to indulge thoughts and feelings that are destructive. If in your attitude you attack yourself or assault your spouse, you can repent by refusing to feed the harmful thought. Repentance means that you turn away from destructive impulses and attitudes you use to manage the pain of neglect and assault and that you face hurt from the spiritual strength of your redeemed heart.

If on a beautiful summer evening you ask your wife to go for a walk with you and she says, "Why would I want to ruin a great night by spending time with you?" you will likely feel a sting that cries for relief. You could manage your pain by despising her for her cruelty or by telling yourself what a loser you are that even your wife wants nothing to do with you. While you may feel some relief, both ways of managing your pain are fueled from a corrupt heart. Repentance requires that you indulge neither attitude. Rather you turn away from destructive impulses and acknowledge the pain of disappointment without attacking yourself or your spouse. This requires courage and the wisdom to suffer in a way that leads to life instead of death.

FORGIVENESS

Jean Valjean had a nemesis whose life mission, perhaps like yours or your spouse's, was to destroy Valjean's life by finding him and giving him the "justice" due him. Despite clear evidences of Valjean's transformed heart, Inspector Javert viewed him as a vermin that had no right to exist. "Once a thief; always a thief," he said. But Valjean loved him. He understood. Valjean sorrowed for the hatred that consumed Javert and robbed him of life.

Remember, God wins in the end. Though it may not always seem so, love is more powerful than hate. Turning the other cheek, going the extra mile, and calling another to goodness is the way of love. The Source of all forgiveness thought it so important to forgive that he allowed himself to be tortured in order for forgiveness to occur. You cannot thrive without a commitment to a lifestyle of forgiveness. Your heart can be too easily darkened by tolerating the cancer of unforgiveness.

One of the most astonishing stories of forgiveness can be found in the book *Left to Tell: Discovering God Amidst the Rwandan Holocaust* by Immaculée Ilibagiza, a woman who lost most of her family in the senseless, evil butchery of the Rwandan genocide. She realized the battle for her heart, devoted herself to repenting of dark thoughts, and trusted God to give her the strength to live a life of forgiveness. She was given an opportunity to meet and have her way with the most sadistic of her family's killers. Having spent hours in spiritual warfare and preparation, she came face-to-face with the man who had wounded her heart with unspeakable wickedness. She wrote:

His dirty clothing hung from his emaciated frame in tatters. His skin was sallow, bruised, and broken: and his eyes were filmed and crusted. His once handsome face was hidden beneath a filthy, matted beard; and his bare feet were covered in open, running sores.

I wept at the sight of his suffering. Felicien had let the devil enter his heart, and the evil had ruined his life like a cancer in his soul. He was now the victim of his victims, destined to live in torment and regret. I was overwhelmed with pity for the man.

. . . Felician was sobbing. I could feel his shame. He looked up at me for only a moment, but our eyes met. I reached out, touched his hands lightly, and quietly said what I'd come to say.

"I forgive you."[3]

We must ask God to help us see with his eyes.

DISENGAGEMENT

Brokenness, repentance, forgiveness. You're ready—but for what? To return to your spouse and say "All is well, let's kiss and make up"? No. We promised you in the beginning of this book that we're not taking you there. If that should happen, if both you and your spouse are going through this process and both of you are broken, repentant, and forgiving, then *wonderful!* God could have amazing things in store for you in your marriage. That would be incredible. It's our deepest desire that your marriage heal and that you are able to complete, enjoy, and enhance each other as God has designed. We simply know that for many of you your marriage will not heal, at least not now. So if it *is* happening for you and your spouse, there are a hundred books we can find to help you rebuild, retool, and engineer your marriage. But for those of you who are thinking, *It's just not going to happen. I know. I've tried. That's why I am reading this book,* please read on. Because rather than *reengaging* with your spouse, we're going to suggest that you *disengage.*

SETTING YOUR SPOUSE FREE

In order to disengage, you must set your spouse free. "You're free!" Now what does that mean? Freedom means telling your spouse, "You no longer have to change. You don't have to be any more a part of my life than you want to be. You can respond to me however you want. And most of all, I set you free from the burden of having to be the answer to the problems in my life and having to play a role in my life you do not want to play. I'm not telling you that there won't be consequences, but I cannot require that you be somebody you're not. I will never stop caring about you, but I cannot look to you for the life that you are unwilling or unable to give. So I set you free. You no longer have to 'get it.' You're free."

That's radical, isn't it? And part of you is saying, "Whoa, wait a minute, guys. Do you mean that my spouse can now do whatever he or she wants? That I have no requirements, my spouse can come and go whenever he or she wants, spend money, treat me as he or she will and I'm just supposed to accept that?" Hasn't my spouse been doing that anyway? The only change is that you will no longer respond to him or her with your pain or anger. Of course, you want to be loved and respected, and if your spouse does not treat you and your marriage responsibly, he or she may have to face consequences. But the consequences will no longer be your expressions of disapproval, cries of pain, whining, pleading, or scolding. While you'll still have to deal with how your spouse treats you, your responses will no longer be rooted in attempts to change your spouse to meet your needs or desires.

So setting your spouse free means that you say, "I give you the right to want what you want, think what you think, view life the way you view it, and respond to life the way you want to respond. I give you that right without passing judgment on you. I accept who you are, even though I know you are not offering what I long for. So you are free to not have to be who I want or need you to be because you can't be that person. You can't be someone you're not."

Accepting that your spouse is who he or she is, doesn't mean you will tolerate everything he or she does. Apparently, to some very abusive people, what they do and how they mistreat their spouses makes sense to them. You need to accept that it does make sense. That doesn't mean that you will tolerate the behavior. That's going to be your choice. "I no longer argue against who you are. I accept that you are who you are. It's done. I will continue to try to understand how you see things so I can accept you at deeper levels."

Does this mean you never talk about your marriage, the difficulties, or about the way he or she affects you? Do you stop hoping he could become more loving? No, it doesn't mean that at all. But what it does mean is that at your very core, the inner part of you, you do not need or require your spouse to be anything other than he or she is or that your spouse see things in any other way than how he or she does. Our hope is that your heart continues to be transformed. We hope you are asking and offering good things in your relationship, and that your spouse will see good changes and lovingly respond to you. But as we have emphatically stated, you have no guarantee he or she will. It is not the goal of the thriving heart to try to get a certain favorable response from your spouse. You are not checking your mate out to see if he or she gets your point.

"What?" you say. "Are you asking me to give up on my spouse? Don't you believe that God could change my spouse? Am I just supposed to settle?" This has nothing to do with settling or giving up on your spouse or your marriage. Our answer to you is to have *wisdom*. You see, you can no longer be naive. That's not allowed. It's not permitted. Naiveté got you to where you are now. We're not saying you should believe your spouse will never change. We are saying you would be really foolish if you refused to learn from the life experiences God has allowed you. You must accept that you have become aware of who your spouse *is*. For now be less concerned about *why* she or he is that way or what your spouse could be like if he or she would only "get it." *"I don't fully understand why you relate to me the way you do, but I do understand this is the way you are and you're not willing or able to change. I'm not confused about that anymore."* This is a critical point. Let's look at how David used his knowledge of who his enemy was, exercised wisdom, and made a difficult choice.

There is a great story in 1 Samuel regarding Saul, the first king of Israel, and David, the man who would eventually take his place. Saul, who had it all, became insanely jealous of David, who had even more in terms of giftedness, achievement, and popularity. Saul drove David out of town and went after him with three thousand of his best-trained soldiers. He was so filled with hatred that he wanted to squash David like a bug. On two occasions, David had the chance to turn the tables and kill Saul, but he didn't.

On one of the occasions, Saul went into a cave to relieve himself. He slipped off his robe and did his business, not realizing he had stumbled into a death trap, the place where David and his men were hiding out. David's men saw this as a sign that God had served Saul to him on a platter and wanted David to kill him. David said he wouldn't kill him because he was God's anointed king. But David did cut a tassel off Saul's robe. When Saul left the cave, David came out and showed him and his men the tassel. He told him he could have killed him and saved his own life, but he didn't. Saul responded with what appears to be brokenness. He wept, asked if David could ever forgive him, and called David his "son." He said that God should bless him for what he did and that David was greater than he was. On a second occasion he even asked David to rejoin him.

But David, rather than reengaging, disengaged. Why? Remember we've not been focusing on behavior, emotions, or words. We have been focusing on the heart. Christ said he didn't entrust himself to men because he knew what was in men's hearts, as he expressed in the gospel of John:

> Now when he was in Jerusalem at the Passover Feast, many believed in his name when they saw the signs that he was doing. But Jesus on his part did not entrust himself to them, because he knew all people and needed no one to bear witness about man, for he himself knew what was in man. (John 2:23-25)

David, though I'm sure he was moved by Saul's display, did not trust Saul's heart. Why? Because David refused to be naive. He had gained wisdom by being with Saul and by seeing his tirades, his inconsistencies, and his ups and downs. There was no way he was going to trust what Saul said or did. He knew what was in Saul's heart. Even though Saul clearly said he had sinned and wouldn't try to harm David anymore, he gave no evidence that he even recognized the main issue. Saul's heart was consumed with bitterness and envy that drove him to try to kill David. Until Saul dealt with the darkness of his bad heart, David could never trust him.

So should you think your spouse is as wicked as King Saul? I don't know, but like David with Saul, you need to know who your mate is and make strong decisions. Certainly if your spouse is dangerous to you and could cause you physical or emotional harm, it would be wise for you to disengage until he or she is no longer dangerous. Until you are able to discern that a meaningful change has occurred and healthy relationship is possible, reengagement is not wise. Continuing to relate to a spouse with destructive patterns is foolish.

Let's get back to the issue that we Christians always focus on: *"Look, what about praying, believing that God could change my spouse? Don't you believe that God could change my spouse? You're not asking me to give up on him or her, are you? Are you telling me to just resign myself and settle for what I have?"*

Yes, of course God could change your spouse—if he chose to do so. But aren't you aware, painfully aware, that God does not choose to impose his will in every situation? Does he desire your spouse to change? Yes. But your spouse may have no interest in cooperating with the Spirit's call on his or her heart. Jesus stood outside Jerusalem and said how he longed to have the people come to him but they refused (see Matthew 23:37; Luke 13:34). Could he have forced them to come to him? Of course. He could force the rocks to cry out praises to him if he wanted (see Luke 19:40). But he has not promised he will change your spouse if you believe strongly enough.

Never give up hope, never give up praying, never close your heart to what may be possible in your marriage. *"Though I am willing to accept who you are and give up any agenda to change you, I am not willing to give up my hope for who you could become and what we could have together."* Praying for your spouse to change and having the faith that God is pursuing his or her heart makes sense. Being certain that your prayers will ultimately result in your spouse's changing does not make sense. Putting your life on hold until he or she changes is foolishness. For many of you, for the foreseeable future—several months to many years—your spouse is going to be who he or she has been, except possibly somewhat disturbed and unsettled by the changes in you. But in wisdom, you need to disengage.

Now you may ask what it means to disengage. *"What should I disengage from? Are you talking about divorce or separation?"* No, not at all. First of all you need to disengage from the destructive patterns in your marriage. This is where we urge you to go to a counselor and talk through some of the specific harmful patterns your marriage has. Your marriage has arrived at "Terms of Engagement." Your spouse may want you to play a role, such as a mother or father, so he or she can be a little boy or girl who doesn't have to take responsibility and make decisions. Or your spouse may want you to be a child whose job is to affirm him and give him authority over your life. Or she may want nothing at all except to basically be left alone. Your spousse may play games such as always making you prove yourself to him or her. Any opinion that differs from your spouse's may have to be justified, explained, and defended. The terms of engagement in a difficult marriage usually has one spouse blaming the other spouse for all their problems.

Throughout this book we have tried to illustrate different roles, types, and ways of interacting that are evidences of difficult marriages. We urge you to do the work of identifying the destructive patterns in your marriage and disengage from them. Again, you may need the help of an insightful counselor or friend to help you see some of the patterns that are destructive.

As you attempt to disengage in your marriage, allow yourself to be guided by a single critical thought: You are not saying your spouse is your enemy. You are not against your spouse. You are not trying to make your spouse out to be a monster, giving him or her horns and a pitchfork. If you do this, you are yielding ground to the Evil One. What you want to be guided by is this statement: *"I want something better for us!* What you are offering me is not good. What you are asking of me is not what I want to give you. I've clarified; I'm not confused. I am rejecting what you are offering. I will be in prayer that you are willing to develop with me a better way. But if you won't, my life is not over. If you won't, I am going to be willing to embrace what is possible with you and accept that there is much you will not offer. So I must disengage from all the destructive qualities of our relationship. I am free to reengage and, as I grow and develop, engage from strength and not from weakness.

How you want to use me—exploit, save, neglect—is YOUR business.

How I allow you to engage me—complete, enjoy, enhance—is MY business.

I will be responsible to do the work to define what love looks like.

I will not let you define me or prescribe what I offer you or want from you."

DISENGAGING FROM YOUR NEGATIVES

Disengagement occurs both on the outside and on the inside. The outside has to do with communication, activities, and roles played. The inside has to do far more with the heart. Let's take a look at what it means to repent in the context of disengaging. Scripture talks about the negative attitudes of the heart:

And he said, "What comes out of a person is what defiles him. For from within, out of the heart of man, come evil thoughts, sexual immorality, theft, murder, adultery, coveting, wickedness, deceit, sensuality, envy, slander, pride, foolishness. All these evil things come from within, and they defile a person." (Mark 7:20-23)

See to it that no one fails to obtain the grace of God; that no "root of bitterness" springs up and causes trouble, and by it many become defiled. (Hebrews 12:15)

You want to disengage from the corruption in your heart. This will be very hard when your marriage continues to cause you pain. Remember where we have located the battle. It's not in your spouse; it's in your heart. Who is the real enemy? It's not your spouse; it's the Evil One. You need to disengage from the dark sentiments you have. This is where the real battle is taking place. You're not going to be able to do this by yourself: You will need prayer and God's strength. Pray for a clean heart, as David did. Ask if there is another way to go, as Valjean did. These are prayers that God will answer. These are prayers that God will bless. Pray God will help you to not recount over and over again all the ways your spouse has not loved you, all the ways you have been hurt. Seek help to bury bitterness and give your desires for vengeance to the Lord. *The major part of disengaging is disengaging from every negative thought, attitude, and emotion that you have toward your spouse, whatever diminishes or lessens him or her.* When you are driving down the street, going into a store, going to work, lying in bed at night, sitting next to him or her in church, repent of the corruption in your heart. Disengage. This doesn't mean that you say it's okay to be mistreated and not respected. Rather, it means that you no longer allow it to corrupt your heart and control your life.

Back in my New York restaurant days, a troubled woman would have lunch regularly in the restaurant where I worked. She would tell me of the horrific ways her husband treated her and of the pain he was causing her. Day after day she would recount stories of disrespect and neglect. One day she came in, very distraught, and said, "Do you know what he did? He shot me! In the neck!"

"What?"

"Yes, he shot me. You don't believe me? Look!" She pulled the collar of her shirt down to expose a wound that could have been caused by a bullet. But I saw that the wound was not bandaged; it was an old scar. A question immediately popped into my mind.

"How long has it been since you have seen your husband?"

"Twelve years."

"Where does he live?"

"In New Orleans."

I thought she was still married to and living with him and that all the fights she had been describing had happened recently. What I realized was that the negative thoughts, feelings, and energies she kept alive kept her connected to her husband. She stayed engaged with her former husband through dark thoughts and attitudes housed in a heart that had been corrupted. I can assure you she would never thrive while her heart remained corrupted. She remained connected to her former husband through negatives.

Here are some practical guidelines to help you disengage from internal corruption. Challenge your heart to allow:

- No criticism
- No tolerance for bitterness, anger, etc.
- No participation in negative talk about your spouse
- No using the kids
- No whining

And to:

- Give up all efforts to show your spouse your pain
- Give up all efforts to change your spouse (more on this in the next chapter)
- Do not interpret everything your spouse does in a negative light
- Practice forgiveness as a way of life

RECLAIMING DESIRES — AN ALIVE HEART

The thief comes only to steal and kill and destroy. I came that they may have life and have it abundantly. (John 10:10)

The thief has come to steal many things. Some of them are the godly thirsts and expressions of your good heart, and he has used your marriage as a weapon against you. Take them back. Reclaim them. In chapter 3, we learned about the healthy thirsts God has placed in your good heart. Your knowledge of them will help you rediscover them underneath your pain.

You wouldn't be suffering if you didn't want something, right? By now we hope you have been doing the hard work of clarifying what you long to receive and desire to offer. Those desires are buried underneath each experience of pain. Rather than focusing all your energy on the pain, move past the pain and discover the desire. It's yours. Reclaim it. Embrace your healthy, good desires. Remember that Christ called us to himself on the basis of our deepest desires: "On the last day of the feast, the great day, Jesus stood up and cried out, 'If anyone thirsts, let him come to me and drink'" (John 7:37).

As you feel the pain in the wound, ask yourself what your best desire is. Embrace the healthy longings of your good heart because they are in danger of being distorted, deadened, or corrupted by wounds.

For example, Adriana, whom we discussed in chapter 7, experienced the wounds of neglect and being orphaned. She was left with questions as to whether or not she would ever be able to offer herself in the way she was designed. She felt foolish when thinking about romantic ideals and cynical when watching a movie where a man professed love to a woman. She was losing the belief in her good heart that her longings and desires were healthy. But they were central to who she was as a person. To strip away hope or tarnish them with bitterness would rob her of the beauty and dignity God gave her.

When cynicism was present in her heart she'd ask herself what she'd like to be able to believe about a man's pledge of love. Her answer was that her heart yearned for the sort of integrity and love a good man could give her. That admission was painful because it was associated with the pain of being neglected by the man who was in a position to offer her what she desired. Rather than give in to the pain and deaden her heart, Adriana also accepted that this side of heaven, her desire would be associated with suffering. Since her longings were an essential part of who she was, she refused to let them die. This is not to say she walked around with a childish, romantic fantasy clouding her head. No. But by finding her desire under her pain, she held a hope that God would use that desire for good. She knew that her bitterness would take her in a different direction, one where there was no life. She committed to praying for the strength to resist the pull toward cynicism. She knew that if she allowed her heart to be alive, she would be alive to many positive experiences in life.

As you move through the darkness in your heart and disengage from the destructive ways of engaging, begin reclaiming desires in the chambers of your heart. Rediscover your good heart under your pain. As Valjean felt the astonishing love of the great bishop, he realized that while his heart longed for vengeance, it was not designed to take from others with no regard for the harm done them. He saw that his heart was designed for a noble purpose: to love with purity, to be part of a purpose that made a substantial difference for good in someone else's life, and to be faithful, true, and honest, even if it cost him.

We urge you to spend time with the Lord reviewing desires in the chambers of your heart, saying that the lights will be on. You will allow yourself to want to enter into someone else's heart and have that someone enter into yours, to desire to move forward with meaning and purpose in your life, and to define that purpose and live it.

Now, we are aware that by allowing yourself to be alive again in the chambers of your soul, not only will you feel anticipation, hope, and healthy desire, but the awareness of unfulfilled desires will also cause an ache for what you don't have. *"Why should I desire what I can never have?"* It's true that you may never know the joy of one-flesh completion. You may not ever know what it is like for someone to join with you and complete you in unity or to have a spouse who will allow you to fully enjoy and enhance you. But it's also true that keeping that very desire alive will make it possible for you to thrive.

CHAPTER 10

The Thriving Heart

You have gotten this far in this book because you are in a difficult marriage and do not want to divorce or follow the "Happily Ever After" or "Noble Misery" paths. Perhaps you are thinking what you have read so far makes sense and offers hope, but you're still not convinced you can thrive if your spouse doesn't change and your marriage remains painful. It feels so hard and so lonely. You may be thinking you don't have what it takes. You're just you and not some sort of "super Christian." While your journey may not be easy, and at times you will feel you are all alone, thriving is possible. There is hope. You don't have to journey alone.

Do you remember the three critical questions we discussed in chapter 2?

1. Do you know what you want to receive and offer?
2. Do you know if what you want is good?
3. Do you know how to keep your heart alive and good when you are disappointed?

The person who has moved beyond survival and has begun to thrive has wrestled with the first two questions and, having repented of corruption, reclaimed the healthy desires in his or her good heart. He or she is determined to never allow the pain of the marriage to take him or her back into darkness. In this chapter we will grapple more fully with the third question. As we do, keep in mind that without wisdom it is not possible to thrive, to keep your heart alive in the face of ongoing disappointment, running the race set before you. By exercising wisdom you can discover how in Christ you can learn to *thrive* and live well even if your marriage remains difficult and your spouse never changes.

In chapter 1 we said wisdom doesn't require that you master a set of technical skills, but rather that you enter a path guided by exercising core convictions. These convictions include:

1. **Marriage means partnering with God.** Holding a belief that God is in it. He loves you and your spouse and is molding and shaping you.

2. **Marriage is bigger than you.** Maintaining a conviction that marriage is worth giving yourself to no matter the cost.

3. **Marriage requires honesty.** Possessing a willingness to relentlessly pursue truth about your self, your spouse, and the state of your marriage.

4. **The battle is in the heart.** Having a passion to maintain integrity of heart and keep hope alive.

These four convictions working together give you a foundation from which you can set wise direction and make prudent decisions when faced with ongoing difficulties in your marriage. Much of what we have discussed has come from the conviction that marriage requires honesty. We will review that conviction and discuss how it and the other three will give you the wisdom to thrive.

MARRIAGE REQUIRES HONESTY

You have been honest about the state of your marriage and the condition of your heart. It is not possible to thrive if you are living under the deception that your marriage or your heart is better or worse than it actually is. Honesty has compelled you to explore what is being asked for and offered in your marriage. You've realized that some of what you want has come from a good heart and some from a bad heart. Because you have been willing to pursue truth, you have accepted who your spouse is and that he or she poses difficulties, many of which are rooted in limited capacities or destructive ways of relating. Integrity has called you to own your issues and the ways you contribute to your marital difficulties. Honesty has required you to accept your own limitations and selfishness. You are committed to deepening your ability to understand what is true about why you do what you do, not allowing yourself to be dishonest about the agendas of your heart.

MARRIAGE IS BIGGER THAN YOU

Marriage is bigger than you. The meaning of marriage transcends what you get out of it, whether you are happy or sad, content or discontent. Many people say they remain in a difficult marriage because they made a vow or entered into a covenant relationship. This implies that the reason for staying in a marriage is not the value of marriage but the value of a commitment or a vow. Does a person refuse to have an affair simply because he or she promised faithfulness to a spouse? If that is the primary reason then the spouse is likely to feel very proud of their choice to remain faithful. But if the partner believes in the sacredness of sexual intimacy and celebration with the one with whom he or she has become one flesh before God, having sex with another person will not make sense. A promise may serve as a reminder, but is not a basis for marital faithfulness.

It's not enough to say you are staying committed to your marriage because you have made a vow before God and are going to keep it no matter what. While honoring a commitment sounds noble, it has a martyr-ish feel to it and may have more to do with your sense of self-respect than valuing marriage. It doesn't usually lead to the sort of powerful conviction that frees a person to thrive despite ongoing difficulties.

In order to hang in and stay committed in an imperfect marriage, you need more than a vow. What you need is a deeply held conviction or belief in the value of marriage that *compels* marital allegiance without requiring happiness. A thriving spouse firmly believes in what he or she has committed himself or herself to. God has designed marriage to represent the value of an eternal relationship. Your marriage is intended to be a picture of Christ's marriage to his bride, the church. Thriving despite does not emerge from a slavish commitment to a vow you wish you had never taken. No, what is needed is not resignation to a burdensome commitment but the passion of a brokenhearted lover who refuses to abandon a belief in the value of marriage or his or her spouse. This conviction results in a determination to honor God and marriage by not allowing a difficult marriage to defeat you. Instead of divorcing or just surviving, you will be compelled to find a way to thrive while remaining loyal to your difficult marriage and spouse. Difficult spouses cannot limit their husband's or wife's ability to thrive, including the willingness to respond to them with a bold love. If you believe in the value of marriage and the idea that it's bigger than you, then you will understand that your marriage doesn't exist to meet your needs or requirements. In order to thrive in a difficult marriage, you need to yield to what it asks of you.

Since we have been privileged to work with missionaries both on the field and at home, let's use them as an example. People become missionaries for many reasons, some good and some bad. Some like the adventure of a different culture, while others are escaping problems and trying to find an identity. I (Mike) have met missionaries who are motivated only by their "call" and go out of duty and obligation. But I have known some very special ones who are on the mission field because they passionately believe in the work God is doing in a country and have given their life to the cause.

Pakistan had a catastrophic earthquake in 2005 that left 75,000 people dead and over 3.3 million homeless with almost no resources to help them recover. The death and loss was unbearable. Christian missionaries were among the first to arrive at the disaster scene, some whose homes and hospitals were damaged by the earthquake. Many lost dear friends as well as Christian colleagues. In the immediate aftermath, some of the only help they could give was to weep with those who were weeping. For most of the missionaries, the efforts to provide aid and minister to the souls of those who were devastated took a severe toll on them physically, emotionally, and spiritually, requiring everything they had to give. When I asked one person about the severe price he and his family were paying for their work, he looked at me with strong eyes and said he only wished he had more strength because the need was so great. He told me he came to Pakistan because he believed in the work God was doing there. His comfort level was of little consequence to him. He was thriving because he had grown into the sort of man who was willing to offer whatever the work required of him, until he had nothing left to give.

So it is in a difficult marriage. Your belief in marriage will lead you to ask God to stretch you into the sort of person who can do what it asks of you. Remember, by the way, your focus is not on yielding to what your spouse requires of you; it is on developing the strengths needed to face the difficulties your marriage asks of you. You will not be able to do this without God's help.

Marriage Means Partnering with God

Likewise the Spirit helps us in our weakness. For we do not know what to pray for as we ought, but the Spirit himself intercedes for us with groanings too deep for words. And he who searches hearts knows what is the mind of the Spirit, because the Spirit intercedes for the saints according to the will of God. And we know that for those who love God all things work together for good, for those who are called according to his purpose. For those whom he foreknew he also predestined to be conformed to the image of his Son, in order that he might be the firstborn among many brothers. (Romans 8:26-29)

The subtitle of Gary Thomas's book *Sacred Marriage* asks the question "What if God designed marriage to make us holy more than to make us happy?"[1] Could this be true? Could God be allowing the Enemy to attack your heart through your painful marriage because he is trying to shape and mold you into a person who has the character of his Son? Would you consider that your suffering is not without purpose?

In his study on Romans 8, Tim Keller quotes a statement John Newton made years ago: "Everything is necessary that he sends; nothing can be necessary that he withholds."

This passage has a specific application for those struggling in a difficult marriage. "Groaning" comes from deep within the chambers of the soul. The groaning occurs when you realize you passionately long for satisfaction of desires, relief of pain, and strength to live with integrity. Only when you come to the end of yourself, having exhausted your strength, and realize you are only too human will you sense the Spirit groaning within you. And then you will know you are not alone. You will begin to understand that God is searching the depths of your heart in order to move you past the taunts of the Enemy who assaults your soul, wanting to pull you into the darkness of shame and bitterness. He is committed to use the suffering you experience as a result of marital wounds and your own failures in order to shape your heart and nature into the character of his own Son. It is when you draw on the good heart God is developing within you that you will be able to meet the challenges your marriage presents and still thrive.

It is encouraging to know that when you allow your spirit to groan with his Spirit, he never leaves you. As you allow these truths to become a core conviction within you, they will provide you the wisdom to thrive knowing you are never alone.

THE BATTLE IS IN THE HEART

You have learned of the great battle that is taking place in your heart. If you remain convinced that the main problem in your marriage is how your spouse neglects or mistreats you, divorce or the "Happily Ever After" and "Noble Misery" paths are your best solutions. But if you have developed the core conviction that the real issue is that the Enemy is using your marital pain to destroy you, while God is utilizing it to transform your heart, you will have the wisdom to learn how to thrive. This conviction allows you to say,

> I can be honest about the pain you cause, but I will not go down that dark tunnel of self-hatred or bitterness toward you. My heart will be alive and good, though not without grief and sorrow. Though I will no longer determine what I do or say by how you respond to me, my heart will remain open to future possibilities with you and our marriage.

WINNING THE BATTLE FOR YOUR HEART

Only God can help you make sense of your suffering. The good news is that you really can thrive and live well despite a difficult marriage. The bad news is that you will not do that without pain. Ongoing suffering will be part of your journey. It is clear that suffering is a part of life. Those who live to avoid suffering either become adept at creating and believing in a fantasy world, avoiding reality, or they live so frivolously and superficially that it is impossible to have any meaningful connection with them. Unfortunately, we live in a culture that has the lowest tolerance for pain of any in history, so you are at a great disadvantage when it comes to finding a way to embrace ongoing suffering in a difficult marriage and believing that you will have the ability to thrive.

Paul helps us with a couple of key concepts from 2 Corinthians. In 2 Corinthians 6:10, Paul wrote that the apostles were *"sorrowful, yet always rejoicing"* (emphasis added). He said he was able to know sorrow because he lived in a difficult world filled with suffering, while at the same time he could experience life in such a way that he found joy. Sounds schizophrenic, doesn't it? So the first concept we want you to chew on is that you can be happy and sad in your marriage—at the same time! That means you don't insist that your marriage be pain free in order for you to thrive. Just because your marriage is difficult and causes you to suffer, you don't have to wake up every morning with despair and sadness because it feels like your marriage is defeating your heart. Rather, Paul was suggesting that (and we know this is a tough, abstract concept) you can wake up feeling "down" from the conflicts of the previous night and at the same time feel "up" as you think about getting into your day. It's a paradox. It's not "either or" sorrow or joy, it's "both and," which is very hard to grasp. We are sorrowful and at the same time rejoicing.

I (Mike) have already mentioned the death of our brother, Mark. Mark died in November of 1990. In June of 1990, our second child, Emily, was born. I recall sitting on the couch in our living room one evening in October of that year after I had just received news that Mark's condition had worsened. I was fighting to not sink into a consuming despair. Emily was at the stage when she was cooing, making eye contact, and blowing bubbles. I remember sitting with this new life, and the pain was nearly overwhelming as I wrestled with inescapable awareness that my kid brother was in physical agony and torment, exercising all his spiritual and physical strength in a futile fight for life. I was helpless to resolve his battle. As tears went down my cheeks, I sat with Emily on the couch, bouncing her on my knee while she cooed and bubbled and smiled with a joy of life that moved into my heart and set up camp right next to the tent of sorrow for my brother. I remember feeling like I was crazy: delighting in the incredible joy, innocence, and beauty of my daughter and torn apart over the demise of my brother. I couldn't make sense of what I was experiencing. It just *was*. I had to embrace both contrasting realities, living in paradox.

LIVING WITH THE REALITY THAT YOU WANT MORE

What do you do when the chambers of your soul are alive, you cry out with longing, and, at best, you experience mild satisfaction or often stinging rejection? The answer Christians give is to take it to the Lord. He satisfies all our needs. He fulfills our deepest longings. While this is true, it doesn't mean the experiences of being exploited, consumed, or betrayed no longer hurt. The Lord doesn't wrap his arms around a person at night and unite with her in loving ecstasy until her body is satisfied. You see, we aren't to think that our experience of God is intended to supply complete and utter satisfaction of all our longings. When Jesus told the woman at the well that if she drank from the living water he provided she would never thirst again, did he mean that she would never have needs, never have desires, never feel an emptiness of any kind? I doubt it. What we believe he meant is that she would taste the real thing, the authentic source of life, and she would never thirst, at her deepest level, for substitutes that could not satisfy. But she hadn't reached the ultimate experience life could bring and so never feel emptiness. That will happen in heaven. In this existence we get the Spirit as a pledge of the fullness that we will know in eternity.

In 2 Corinthians 5 Paul said we exist in a temporary structure that we know is not permanent. It's not something we can feel secure in, and the normal state of being is to *groan*, to long for the permanent, complete, and ultimate structure. The groaning Paul talked about suggests that there is deep suffering and torment in the soul as it realizes it craves so much more satisfaction than a fallen world can provide. In fact, Paul said the whole creation groans, waiting in anticipation of what's to come.

Maturity is developed as we begin to recognize that our souls long for more than our spouses are able or willing to provide and we learn to "groan" in a way that leads to life. As C. S. Lewis said in *Mere Christianity*, "If I find a desire which no experience in this world can satisfy, the most probable explanation is that I was made for another world."[2] While it seems absurd to talk about a good way to suffer, the truth is there is a *groaning that leads to life.* Yes, there is a groaning that leads to death, but the groaning Paul encouraged is one that clarifies and brings perspective as to why we are in pain.

James Stockdale was the highest ranking officer in the North Vietnamese Prison Camp, called the "Hanoi Hilton," during the Vietnam war. He lived in torturous, sadistic conditions where men were regularly beaten, couldn't communicate with each other or the outside world, and didn't know when or if they would get out or whether they would live or die. Stockdale knew that he needed to find a way to survive. The term "Stockdale Paradox" developed because of the way he survived his time in the Hanoi Hilton. He said he never gave up his belief that he would someday get out of that prison, while at the same time accepting and finding a way to cope with the most brutal of realities in the prison camp.

This idea is essential for understanding how to thrive while suffering. You must hold on to the faith and hope that someday it's all going to make sense, that there is another day coming that is designed and developed by a Holy God who is good and does not waste pain. One day you will know how God has utilized your sufferings in ways you cannot understand now. The pain caused by the difficulties in your marriage is not meaningless. So you groan through the pain with a joy, hope, and anticipation, a faith and belief that your suffering is not without meaning.

The second part of the Stockdale Paradox is that in light of our hope, it is essential that we face every difficulty life presents. Our hope doesn't cause us to live in fantasy, pretending what we are facing doesn't hurt. Our hope gives us the courage and strength to deal with the dilemmas that come our way: the pain and conflict found in a difficult marriage. The problems don't have to go away for you to thrive, believing that some day this is all going to make sense.

The Gap

Christ also has shown a way to deal with the difficulties in marriage without becoming bitter and without the necessity of building a huge wall between you and your spouse. This is done by understanding how to handle the pain found in "the gap." The battle for your heart centers on the enormous problem of how you choose to address the pain that occurs in the gap between what your heart desires and what is available in your spouse and marriage.

Picture a graph with two vertical lines on it going from 0 to 100 percent. The first line, the desire line, is what you long to offer and receive. If your heart is alive, the desire line is marked at nearly 100 percent. The second line, graphing the percentage of your desires that your spouse is available to fulfill, is called the availability line, the response of your spouse. You will find a significant gap exists between what you long for and what is available. (We could put a third line that would chart the percentage of the desires that your spouse believes he or she is fulfilling in your marriage, a percentage usually much higher than what you believe is available to you, creating an even larger gap.) The battle to keep your heart alive and good is won or lost by how you handle the disappointment and suffering you experience in what we call "the gap."

The solution to living with the gap is becoming willing to bear the burden of the knowledge that there are significant things you crave that are not available in your marriage and that your spouse either doesn't know or doesn't care. Since this is such an important concept and is key in learning how to thrive, we're going to take a little more time to develop this and give you a couple of examples.

The first example comes from our work with helping people thrive even though they have been sexually abused as children. Some sexual abuse therapy methods have as their breakthrough moment a cathartic experience when healing will actually occur, a confrontation with the abuser. Let's say a woman in her midthirties has finally been strong and honest enough to face the damage done by her father when he sexually abused her as a young child. As she works through her pain, gains strength, conquers fear, and reclaims self, she is told that in order to be completely healed and reclaim her strength and dignity as a woman, it is necessary for her to go to her father and confront him with his sin. She must tell him of her pain, hopefully reconcile, and emerge from that encounter very different from the incidents of abuse. She will emerge with power and strength and dignity. While many say they have greatly benefited from such confrontations, we have found that the experience of people who have attempted to do this has not been ultimately good.

Let's say the abusive father gets it, takes full responsibility, has read books on abuse, and is willing to hear about the pain he has caused his daughter. When his daughter sits with him and begins to recount the suffering the abuse cost her — promiscuity, eating disorders, fear of her husband, lack of pleasure, depression, years lost, fear of having children — she hopes in her heart that her father will understand, will enter into her pain, and will offer a repentance and compassion that helps to restore her broken heart and perhaps even their relationship. But what she finds is that at his most caring and compassionate best, he is able to comprehend only a miniscule portion of what she has experienced as a result of his abuse. He may weep with her and tell her he's sorry, yet something in her soul is saying, "Yes, but I don't think you quite get it. I don't think you fully understand." She realizes there is a gap between what she longs for him to know and what he is capable of knowing.

He wasn't with her; he didn't go through the dark nights, the emptiness, the feelings of betrayal. Those were her experiences and hers alone. What she must do in order to reconcile or even to go on with her life without bitterness is to take all that he can't know or understand, put it in a large sack, put the sack on her back, and, with her courageous, wise, transformed heart, relieve him of the burden of having to "get it." If she insists that he get it, she will always feel hurt, misunderstood, even reabused, and will therefore justify distance and hostility. *So the forgiver must bear the burden of the offender's not understanding the depth of the offense.* He never will. In *Bold Love,* Dan Allender taught that the purpose of confrontation is to bring the perpetrator to an awareness of his need for the same grace that has set you free from the shame and guilt of your sins.

The second example is about Christ. We are the perpetrator, confronted with our sins, and we don't "get it." He "gets it" and was willing to take our offenses on his back without requiring that we fully understand what we have done to him. We can't. "But God shows his love for us in that while we were still sinners, Christ died for us" (Romans 5:8).

We don't have a clue, not really, as to the enormity of what the Cross is all about. He knows that and took action anyway. We also can't even begin to understand what Christ allowed himself to endure for us. It takes great strength, great wisdom, and great humility to say to your spouse, "You don't get it, but that's okay because I get that you don't get it. You don't have to get it. I'll bear the burden of what you don't get." This is what Jesus has said to his beloved and what he lived out on the cross.

With the wisdom of Christ you realize that you must absorb the pain in the gap. You set your spouse free while you bear the burden of knowing what he or she cannot or refuses to know. You must be willing to say, "It's okay that you don't get it. It hurts, it stings, and I feel lonely, but I won't make you pay. I won't go off into a sulk. I won't sink into depression. I'll carry the pain, absorb it, and move forward." This is the way God provides for you to deal with the gap in your marriage.

Another note of caution: We are not suggesting that you allow yourself to just stand and take punches. While you need to be willing to carry the pain, you can also choose, out of wisdom, to find ways to limit access to your heart. This is especially true if your spouse is acting from a bad heart and is not *for* you and your marriage. In dealing with the gap and facing the deep pain and disappointment experienced in a difficult marriage, you refuse to act from a corrupt, surviving heart and choose to respond from your good, wise heart. As you do this, you become free to come to the third element of thriving.

By the way, by absorbing the pain found in the gap, you are already thriving. You may say, "Thriving? Man, that sounds like work. That sounds heavy!" Yes, it is. And it takes courage. Did you ever think that running a marathon was easy? Ask me (Chuck). I've run over fifty of them. There are no easy marathons. Why do I keep running them? Because there is something rich and satisfying about conquering those twenty-six miles. There is a joy as I thrive through the effort and pain of a marathon. Every one of them costs me something. Please don't resist that concept anymore; embrace it. It is a liberating concept because any honest look at Scripture will tell you that the way God causes his people to thrive is to put them in uncomfortable places where they must find ways to not give in to weakness, develop new strengths, and exercise great wisdom.

REENGAGEMENT: THRIVING IN THE POSSIBLE

Now we are going to go a step further. When you accept the burden of carrying the pain found in the gap, you are free to embrace what is possible, accept what is not possible, and thrive both in and out of your marriage.

A great example of this is found in the scene of Jesus and his closest friends, Peter, James, and John in the Garden of Gethsemane:

> He went back and found them asleep. He said to Peter, "Simon, are you sleeping? Couldn't you stay awake for one hour? Stay awake, and pray that you won't be tempted. You want to do what's right, but you're weak." (Mark 14:37-38, GW)

Jesus had brought these men into the torment of his soul and asked them to strengthen him by praying for him while he agonized with the Father. He separated himself to pray to the Father, counting on his friends to sustain him in prayer. When he stopped praying and came back to them, they had fallen asleep. The gap between what he hoped for and what was available was enormous. Imagine the pain he must have felt when his friends let him down when he needed them the most. So how did he respond to them? He didn't avoid confronting them with their failure, but he didn't tell them about his need or pain. It must have been clear to him that they had a limited ability to understand the depth of what he needed from them. He absorbed the pain of being let down and changed what he asked of them. He no longer asked them to enter his pain and encourage him through pain (what was not possible). He asked them to pray for what they could understand, their need to resist being tempted to give in to their weakness (what was possible). Christ adjusted because he had the wisdom to know what was available and not press for what was not available. Of course, he did this while entering into the greatest pain and suffering any being has ever experienced.

Thriving requires you to understand that, unlike Christ, you also act like the disciples, being more focused on yourself than your spouse, accepting you also have limitations. You are aware of what you cannot offer to your spouse and how he has a gap between what he longs for from you and the marriage and what is available. In a healthy marriage you must be strong enough to allow your spouse to be disappointed in you, struggling with his own gap, and yet be wise enough to never give in to demands that you give what you do not have or what is not good. In humility and confession, ask your spouse to embrace that you also are who you are and cannot provide all the things your spouse may desire. Neither of you needs to apologize for who you are not.

For some of you the gap is 90 percent or more. For others the gap may be smaller and more manageable. The work you need to do and, hopefully, have been doing is to come to grips with what is possible in your marriage by studying your spouse, learning from your years of marriage, and knowing your own heart. This is a life task because what is possible changes as people change and time moves on. In keeping your heart alive, you must not allow yourself to be controlled, hurt, and confused by what is not possible. You no longer draw attention to what doesn't happen in your marriage, sending messages of pain and suffering to your spouse or reacting indignantly when you don't get what you want. With wisdom you figure out the areas where you can connect well with your spouse, and you enjoy those times as you embrace what is possible; likewise, you refuse to make them pay for not being able to engage and connect in other areas.

CALLING YOUR SPOUSE TO "MORE"

Never give up on a vision or picture of a redeemed, strong version of what your spouse could grow into. Do this based on your ability to accept who your spouse is so you don't have a vision of who *you* want him or her to be. Remember symbiosis—your spouse is "other" than you. So as you continue to develop a vision of who your spouse could be, you lovingly invite him, draw her, and give him the opportunity to grow and express the strength and beauty God has placed within her. You don't do this out of your own need for a spouse who could fulfill your dreams. Rather you begin calling your mate to strength, beauty, and holiness for him or her, for the marriage, for the family, and for God. You are not asking your spouse to change or grow out of your weakness or out of your own need to be made whole.

Once again you may be thinking you've been given a bait and switch. "You started off saying some marriages remain difficult no matter what, and now you are saying my marriage can be fixed by following your steps. Thanks a lot. I have already tried everything, and I am telling you my spouse is not interested in changing anything. He will keep as far away from me as possible, offering and wanting nothing, or else assault me with all the ways I don't measure up. You're starting to paint a rosy picture, and I don't think I will ever experience deep joy in my marriage."

Don't give up on the rosy picture entirely. As you choose not to react to your spouse from a bad heart and approach your marriage from strength rather than weakness, you are actually in the best place to offer and receive good things. It is also very likely that your pain and confusion kept you from being able to receive or give what is possible in your marriage. What we are suggesting is that while other paths for facing a difficult marriage keep the heart closed, the thriving heart retains hope and actively remains open to the possibility of change. But your life is not put on hold waiting for that change to occur. You allow yourself to thrive and invest your strength and beauty wherever God gives you opportunity. In fact, as you begin to think about it, you will recognize you are already thriving in other areas of your life but have not fully embraced it because you thought you couldn't while your marriage remained difficult.

"So what does this mean, how do I do that?" That's your task. You are now free to do it. Welcome to life. *"Does that mean I have to go back to school and get a career?"* You could do that. *"Does it mean that I have to go on the mission field or find volunteer work?"* You could also do that. But what you want to say is, "My life is no longer on hold, waiting for my marriage to get better. My well-being and ability to thrive in life do not depend on a change in my spouse."

God has relationship and purpose available for you in many places, and you have the privilege of investing your heart, your gifts, and your abilities wherever you think it will matter. You have the privilege and responsibility to offer who you are and engage in life in a way that your beauty and strength are expressed for the benefit of others, and God is thrilled. That may mean that you invest yourself in keeping your house in good repair, providing a place your family is proud of, your kids enjoy, and where you can offer hospitality. Or you may invest yourself on the mission field and do six short-term trips or one three-month trip in a year. Or you may learn to play the guitar for your own pleasure.

You see, what you choose to do isn't nearly as important as your willingness to invest meaning, purpose, and integrity into it. You've done your homework of finding out what is important, what matters to you, and what is good. You begin doing what you do not for the purpose of self-enhancement but to express, for God's glory and the benefit of others, who you are. You need to believe in and define the value and worth of what you do. If your spouse says, "Why are you spending so much time doing that?" or if he or she doesn't notice the effort and care that you have applied to something you are involved with, do not let him or her rob you of the value of what you have done.

Here is the paradox: joy coexisting with sorrow. Of course you will feel a sharp sting if your spouse degrades or ignores the good ways you offer yourself. You may live with the dark cloud of disapproval or even disgust permeating the atmosphere of your home. It's unrealistic to think you wouldn't feel sorrow and grief with ongoing rejection. Yet you can still delight and find joy in the ways you are thriving.

The greatest example we know of this is from the film *The Passion of the Christ*. As Jesus was walking to Gethsemane, having had his body broken through sadistic torture and facing even more pain in the agony he would face on the cross, he encountered his mother, Mary. Rather than letting himself be defined and dominated by what was being done to him, he chose to speak from the purpose and meaning he brought to that event. Rather than saying, "I hurt so badly. They are killing me," he made a stunning statement when he said, "Mother, behold, I make all things new." He knew why he was doing what he was doing, and Satan and all the legions of hell could not make him redefine the purposes of his heart. While this expression is not from Scripture, the writer captured the idea that Christ's circumstances did not define his mission. This is the epitome of living out the Stockdale Paradox, but Christ developed it long before Stockdale existed.

THE ULTIMATE KEY TO THRIVING DESPITE

Now that you have repented of survival strategies, you can know how to handle the suffering and disappointment you experience when you don't find satisfaction for your longings and are committed to thriving despite ongoing pain in your marriage. You are ready for the most powerful aspect of thriving: understanding that it's not all about you; it's about God.

One of the characteristics of deep depression is that the pain of depression causes a person to become very selfish. Life is so difficult for depressed people that they are preoccupied with finding a way to get through each day. They may be consumed with self-hatred for their failures or with anger that no one cares or understands how hard life is for them. Something similar happens to people weighed down by the pain of a difficult marriage. They are consumed with trying to find a way to get their spouses to change, to change themselves to make their spouses happy, or to numb their pain.

Their pain is the centerpiece of their lives, and all they do is determined by it. When you agree to coexist with pain, allowing joy and sorrow to be part of your life, pain begins to have less dominance. You come to live from your good heart for the well-being of your family and God. But you are still you. You are good, bad, ugly, and beautiful. You are strong and weak, wise and foolish. Even with your determination to bring value to what you do, you still can't make it all work. You'll never love as well as you'd like, and you'll never let yourself be loved as much as others would like. The good news is that you don't have to "get it all together." God knows all about "otherness." He knows better than you that though you are like him in some ways, you are not him and will never get it together so you are able to thrive no matter what. He knows you can't journey alone. That's why the ability to thrive occurs when you embrace the Spirit's groaning within you and let God do his thing.

Patty and Dave

Patty and Dave continued counseling for several months. As we went into depth about what each was offering and asking of the other, Patty became aware that much of what she was asking of Dave had been shaped by her experiences with significant men in her life. She had believed it was essential that Dave compliment her appearance and find her attractive. To fulfill that desire she had allowed herself to believe that his need to have frequent sex was because he desired her beauty. She also believed that the best she had to offer him was her body. Isn't that what men always wanted from her? She discovered that the best longings in her heart were to offer him a different sort of beauty.

As the weeks went by, she became vocal with what she believed she and Dave could become. She offered him a beautiful hope for the way they could become honest with how they treated each other and how little they were able to trust. She invited him to explore the truth of what sex was all about for him and related the many other ways she believed he was a strong, adequate man. Dave was intrigued and began to wonder if more was possible for their marriage. He even enjoyed spending time talking and cuddling before and after sex. Patty started coming alive in ways that were wonderful. But Dave got frightened. She wanted to understand why it was important for him to occasionally turn to pornography, especially as they were getting closer and enjoying their times of intimacy.

As she asked him to involve himself with this important issue, he snapped. She was getting too close. All the ways he used to get away were being taken from him. If he agreed to explore his involvement with pornography, he may lose his place to play out his sexual fantasies. That would mean his only area to feel like a man would be with Patty. Because he was still unsure that he had the strength Patty was asking for, he sabotaged counseling and went back to treating Patty as he always had.

Patty was in more pain than when she had started counseling. Her heart was opening up as never before, and she was abandoned. She not only felt betrayed; she experienced death in her marriage. She was a widow who had been rejected and abandoned. Her grief was intense. The longing she felt to continue their good direction was overwhelming. But she refused to beg. She also refused to offer herself as she had before. Dave made her pay. Each demeaning comment he uttered caused her to suffer.

Two years later they were still married. Patty told me that she was no longer on antidepressants, though she still had some dark days. Rather than talking about her marriage, she shared her excitement about the job she had taken with a local investment company. She was learning new things nearly every day and had been offered a promotion after only six months.

Dave never stopped raging at her or pressuring her for sex on demand. He was nearly violent several months ago but was more like a hurt and confused kid recently. His real frustration was that Patty wouldn't fight with him. He accused her of having an affair because that might explain why she wouldn't engage with his destructive offerings. Patty knew better. Her deepest needs were no longer addressed to David. She knew that only Christ knew and loved her in the way she most deeply desired.

What Dave would never understand was that Patty didn't hate him; she loved him. She was prepared to reengage her heart with him if he would only speak from a good heart and ask for the beauty she knew she had to offer. Tragically, David didn't know what he didn't know. He thought he had it all figured out, that his wife had turned into a rejecting, cold woman. What he didn't know was that he lived with a woman who ached to engage with him in a way that would complete them both and honor God. She sorrowed over what she would never experience with him, but at the same time she knew joy in her alive and passionate heart which she freely expressed to many. I'm convinced that Dave's "get even" and "get away" survival strategies will eventually turn him into a bitter old man. I am more sure that Patty will continue to thrive and bring joy to many until the Lord takes her home.

Quite a story—and maybe not the fairy-tale ending we all instinctively want. But Patty's response to her disappointment has made all the difference. By joining with God to fight and win the battle for her heart, the chambers of her soul exude beauty and strength instead of bitterness, despair, pride, or apathy. There is hope! We hope you feel encouraged to not give up, to focus on the real issues of your heart, and to see God as the One to help you flourish while in a painful marriage. It is possible to "thrive despite" a difficult marriage.

"It is God who works in you, both to will and to work for his good pleasure." (Philippians 2:13)

Notes

CHAPTER 2

1. Harvel Hendrix and Helen Hunt, *Receiving the Love You Want* (New York: Atria Books, 2004), 64–67.
2. Oswald Chambers, *Baffled to Fight Better* (Grand Rapids, MI: Discovery House, 1931), 105, 138.

CHAPTER 3

1. John Eldredge, *Journey of Desire* (Nashville, TN: Thomas Nelson, 2000), 29.
2. Larry Crabb, "A Liberating Look at Gender" (Audio Series, New Way Ministries).
3. Crabb, audio series.
4. Dan B. Allender and Tremper Longman III, *Intimate Allies* (Wheaton, Il: Tyndale, 1995), 73.

CHAPTER 7

1. Robert Kellemen, *Soul Physicians* (Taneytown, MD: RPM Books, 2005), 283.

CHAPTER 9

1. Victor Hugo, *Les Misérables,* Musical Version. Claude-Michel Schönberg, Alain Boublil, 1987.
2. Charles Spurgeon, *Morning and Evening* (Geanies House, Scotland Christian Focus Publications, 1994), April 3, Evening.
3. Immaculée Ilibagiza with Steve Erwin, *Left to Tell* (Carlsbad, CA: Hay House, 2006), 204.

CHAPTER 10

1. Gary Thomas, *Sacred Marriage* (Grand Rapids, MI: Zondervan, 2000), 13.
2. C. S. Lewis, *Mere Christianity* (New York: Macmillan, 1943), 120.

About the Authors

MICHAEL MISJA, PhD, BCPCC, is a Christian psychologist and cofounder of North Coast Family Foundation in Cleveland and Akron, Ohio. He has counseled, taught, and spoken on Christian counseling for more than twenty years. In addition to the daily call show he hosted for six years, Michael developed and taught a program in Christian counseling for Moody Extension School for ten years. He has also served as cofounder and clinical director for inpatient and outpatient Christian counseling centers. He and his wife, Lin, found God and were married in New York City, where they were active in the arts and in ministry. They have been married twenty-seven years and have four children.

CHARLES F. MISJA, PhD, is a licensed psychologist and cofounder of North Coast Family Foundation in Cleveland and Akron, Ohio. He has hosted a Christian call-in talk show on several radio stations and has taught at the college and seminary level. Chuck maintains a clinical practice and has been involved with missions work in Brazil for many years. He and his wife, Jackie, are high school sweethearts and have been married thirty-seven years. They have three grown children and six grandchildren. Chuck enjoys running marathons, downhill skiing, and fishing with his grandchildren.

Other marriage titles from NavPress!

Intimacy Ignited
Dr. Joseph Dillow, Linda Dillow, Dr. Peter Pintus, and Lorraine Pintus
978-1-57683-640-8

Looking for more romance in your marriage? A follow-up to the best seller *Intimate Issues*, this book takes you on a verse-by-verse exploration of the Bible's very own manual on sex and intimacy: Song of Solomon. The authors show you how this timeless love poem explains that the secret to great sex in marriage begins with a servant heart.

Rocking the Roles
Robert Lewis and William Hendricks
978-1-57683-125-0

Rocking the Roles examines what the Bible really has to say about the male and female roles. A far cry from the restrictions of the traditional marriage or the formlessness of modern marriage, this approach offers a perfect blend of structure, equality, balance, and beauty.

When I Get Married
Jerusha Clark
978-1-60006-056-4

Many people don't realize how toxic their misconceptions of marriage can be. *When I Get Married* explores ten common topics, including money, sex, love, and life purpose. Learn how to defeat false ideas with biblical truths and come away with renewed joy and hope for what God offers in marriage.

To order copies, call NavPress at 1-800-366-7788
or log on to www.navpress.com.

NAVPRESS